Humble Yourself
The Way to Greatness

by Wendy Bowen, Manifest International
www.manifestinternational.com

COURSE DESCRIPTION & INTRODUCTION: 9 UNITS

This course will bring you into a dynamic revelation of the ways of God's Kingdom. The way up is down. The way to greatness is to humble ourselves before God.

PRAY FOR REVELATION:

Before taking this course, pray and ask the Lord to give you wisdom and revelation as you grow in your knowledge of Him. We are believing with you that the Lord will illuminate His word for you through this course and open your mind to understand the Scriptures and the truth of Jesus like never before.

MANIFEST APPROACH COURSES: MARKETING STRATEGY

The purpose of courses designated as "Approach Courses" is to express the beliefs and way of life God has given to us at Manifest International. As such, this course is an expanded Biblical explanation of our approach to marketing.

Our Marketing Strategy is: "Those who exalt themselves will be humbled, and those who humble themselves will be exalted." (Matthew 23;12.) "Humble yourselves, therefore, under the mighty hand of God so that at the proper time He may exalt you." (1 Peter 5:6.) We trust God to promote and raise us up in His timing. We do not promote ourselves, advertise, or use marketing strategies of this world.

HUMBLE YOURSELF: THE WAY TO GREATNESS, PAPERBACK

Copyright © 2021 Wendy Bowen – ALL RIGHTS RESERVED WORLDWIDE
Manifest International, LLC
ISBN: 978-1-951280-28-4

Cover Design: Don Patton, Image Credit: Designed by evening_tao / Freepik

SCRIPTURE TRANSLATION

Scripture quotations are from The ESV ® Bible (The Holy Bible, English Standard Version®), copyright © 2001 by Crossway, a publishing ministry of Good News Publishers. Used by permission. All rights reserved.

No translation of Scripture is perfect and without slight pollutions of the interpretations of man. The ESV has been selected based upon the fact that it is a word-for-word translation of the original Hebrew, Aramaic, and Greek texts of Scripture using current English language. We value other translations such as the King James (KJV) and New King James (NKJV) versions of Scripture for their accuracy and also New International (NIV) and New Living (NLT) translations for their readability.

All Biblical definitions in this book are from Strong's Hebrew and Greek Lexicon, Gesenius' Hebrew-Chaldee Lexicon, and Thayer's Greek Lexicon.

Cover Design: Don Patton Design – www.donpattondesign.com

Table of Contents

Unit #	Name	Page
Unit One:	The Mindset of Jesus	1
Unit Two:	The Way to Destruction: Pride & Selfish Ambition	9
Unit Three:	God Humbles the Proud & Exalts the Humble	21
Unit Four:	Humble Yourself Before God Part One: Turning	35
Unit Five:	Humble Yourself Before God Part Two: Seeking	51
Unit Six:	Humble Yourself Before Men The Lowest Place	64
Unit Seven:	Humble Yourself in Trials & Suffering	78
Unit Eight:	The Way to Salvation: Abide & Endure to the End	94
Unit Nine:	The Way of Christ: Meekness & Sonship	104

Unit One: The Mindset of Jesus

> Have this mind among yourselves, which is yours in Christ Jesus, who, though he was in the form of God, did not count equality with God a thing to be grasped.
>
> Philippians 2:5-6

A. Jesus Humbled Himself

1. Philippians 2:3-8 - 3 **Do nothing from selfish ambition or conceit**, but in humility count others more significant than yourselves. 4 Let each of you **look not only to his own interests, but also to the interests of others**. 5 Have this mind among yourselves, which is yours in Christ Jesus, 6 who, though he was in the form of God, **did not count equality with God a thing to be grasped**, 7 but **emptied himself**, by **taking the form of a servant**, being born in the likeness of men. 8 And being found in human form, **he humbled himself by becoming obedient to the point of death, even death on a cross.**

    a. Jesus had no ambition of for His own will or reputation. He emptied Himself of His own will and subjected Himself as an obedient slave to the will of God.

   > Emptied: Greek-G2758: *kenoo*: 1. To empty or make empty. 2. To make void, deprive of force, render vain, useless or of no effect. 3. To cause a thing to be seen as empty, hollow, and false.
   >
   > Servant: Greek-G1401: *doulos*: 1. A slave, bondman, or man of servile condition. 2. A person in subjection or subserviency. 3. One who gives themselves up to another's will. Devoted to another, to the disregard of one's own interests.

    i. John 5:19, 30 - 19 So Jesus said to them, "Truly, truly, I say to you, the Son can do nothing of his own accord, but **only what he sees the Father doing**. For whatever the Father does, that the Son does likewise. ... 30 "I can do nothing on my own. As I hear, I judge, and my judgment is just, **because I seek not my own will but the will of him who sent me**.

    ii. John 12:49-50 - 49 For **I have not spoken on my own authority, but the Father who sent me** has himself given me a commandment--**what to say and what to speak**. 50 And I know that his commandment is eternal life. **What I say, therefore, I say as the Father has told me**."

    iii. John 8:28 - 28 So Jesus said to them, "When you have lifted up the Son of Man, then you will know that I am he, and that **I do nothing on my own authority, but speak just as the Father taught me**.

    b. Jesus is God in the flesh but did not abuse God's power or authority for His own agenda. Rather, He used the power and authority of God to demonstrate the agenda of God to show mercy. He was moved with compassion for the lost, the hungry, the sick, the possessed and oppressed. Through the mercy of God and forgiveness of their sins, they were made whole, healed, delivered, and set free.

i. John 6:38 - 38 For I have come down from heaven, **not to do my own will but the will of him who sent me**.
   ii. Matthew 11:4-6 - 4 And Jesus answered them, "Go and tell John what you hear and see: 5 **the blind receive their sight and the lame walk, lepers are cleansed and the deaf hear, and the dead are raised up, and the poor have good news preached to them**. 6 And blessed is the one who is not offended by me."
   iii. John 10:37-38 - 37 **If I am not doing the works of my Father, then do not believe me**; 38 but if I do them, even though you do not believe me, believe the works, that you may know and understand that the Father is in me and I am in the Father."

c. Jesus did not look for glory from men. Many people followed Him and gathered around Him because of the miracles and wanted to make Him king on earth. But rather than allowing man to exalt Him, Jesus proceeded to tell His hardest teaching about eating His flesh and drinking His blood so that they were so repulsed that they no longer followed Him.
   i. John 6:15 - 15 Perceiving then that they were about to come and take him by force to **make him king, Jesus withdrew again to the mountain by himself**.
   ii. John 8:50 - 50 Yet **I do not seek my own glory**; there is One who seeks it, and he is the judge.
   iii. Note: Jesus allowed Himself to be worshipped by those who recognized Him and bowed before Him. BUT He did not demand worship or seek it for His own glorification. His glory came from God and everything He did was for the glory of God.

d. Jesus obeyed God to the point of death out of total righteousness and submission to the will of God. He allowed Himself to be slaughtered as the Lamb of God - crucified as a criminal.
   i. Isaiah 53:7-10 - 7 He was oppressed, and he was afflicted, yet he opened not his mouth; **like a lamb that is led to the slaughter, and like a sheep that before its shearers is silent, so he opened not his mouth**. 8 By oppression and judgment he was taken away; and as for his generation, who considered that he was cut off out of the land of the living, stricken for the transgression of my people? 9 And they made his grave with the wicked and with a rich man in his death, **although he had done no violence, and there was no deceit in his mouth**. 10 Yet **it was the will of the LORD to crush him; he has put him to grief; when his soul makes an offering for guilt**, he shall see his offspring; he shall prolong his days; the will of the LORD shall prosper in his hand.
   ii. Matthew 16:21 - 21 From that time **Jesus began to show his disciples that he must go to Jerusalem and suffer many things** from the elders and chief priests and scribes, **and be killed, and on the third day be raised**.
   iii. John 13:1 - 1 Now before the Feast of the Passover, when **Jesus knew that his hour had come to depart out of this world to the Father**, having loved his own who were in the world, he loved them to the end. [Into washing the disciples feet.]
   iv. Matthew 26:38-39 - 38 Then he said to them, "My soul is very sorrowful, even to death; remain here, and watch with me." 39 And going a little farther he fell on his face and prayed, saying, "My Father, if it be possible, let this cup pass from me; **nevertheless, not as I will, but as you will**."

2. Philippians 2:9-11 - 9 **Therefore God has highly exalted him and bestowed on him the name that is above every name**, 10 so that at the name of Jesus every knee should bow, in heaven and on earth and under the earth, 11 and every tongue confess that Jesus Christ is Lord, to the glory of God the Father.

   a. THEREFORE: It is because of Jesus humility, submission, and obedience that He has the greatest name in all of human history in heaven and on earth.

3. Philippians 2:12-13 - 12 **Therefore**, my beloved, as you have always obeyed, so now, not only as in my presence but much more in my absence, **work out your own salvation with fear and trembling**, 13 for it is **God who works in you, both to will and to work for his good pleasure**.

   a. THEREFORE, we must likewise obey God to work out our salvation through humility and obedience as Jesus demonstrated for us.

B. A Great Name

1. Having a great name has always been important to mankind. A great name is earned through character and/or ability as a person develops a reputation for being a certain way or being capable of doing certain things.

   a. Since ancient times, in every culture, a great name was earned through an established track-record of credibility and character, etc.
      i. A person proved trustworthy in trade and dealings.
      ii. A person proved reliable to follow through with what they said/promised.
      iii. A person proved to be a faithful ally against enemies.

   b. A great name in the wisdom books.
      i. Proverbs 22:1 - 1 **A good name is to be chosen rather than great riches**, and favor is better than silver or gold.
      ii. Proverbs 10:7 - 7 **The memory of the righteous is a blessing**, but the name of the wicked will rot.
      iii. Ecclesiastes 7:1 - 1 **A good name is better than precious ointment**...

   c. Having a great name in the sight of man is not always a good thing in the sight of God.
      i. Genesis 10:8-9 - 8 Cush fathered Nimrod; he was the first on earth to be a mighty man. 9 He was a mighty hunter before the LORD. **Therefore it is said, "Like Nimrod a mighty hunter before the LORD."**
      ii. Luke 16:15 - 15 And he said to them, "You [Pharisees] are those who **justify yourselves before men**, but God knows your hearts. For **what is exalted among men is an abomination in the sight of God**.

2. Example: Abraham: A great name through faith –> 2nd most famous man in history, after Jesus.

   a. Genesis 12:1-3 - 1 Now the LORD said to Abram, "Go from your country and your kindred and your father's house to the land that I will show you. 2 And I will make of you a great nation, and **I will bless you and make your name great**, so that you will be a blessing. 3 I will bless those who bless you, and him who dishonors you I will curse, and in you all the families of the earth shall be blessed."

   b. Abraham was a nomad, living in tents with no permanent home of his own, believing that God was going to give him the land of ten nations, innumerable descendants, and a great name.

3. Example: David: A great name through a heart for God –> 3rd most famous man in history.

   a. 2 Samuel 7:8-9 - 8 Now, therefore, thus you shall say to my servant David, 'Thus says the LORD of hosts, I took you from the pasture, from following the sheep, that you should be prince over my people Israel. 9 And I have been with you wherever you went and have cut off all your enemies from before you. And **I will make for you a great name, like the name of the great ones of the earth**.

   b. David started as a shepherd and runt of his family. Then, he served in Saul's court as a warrior and musician. Then, he wandered for years as a fugitive living in wilderness caves with a band of rebels waiting for it to be his time without taking matters into his own hands to exalt himself or usurp authority. Then, he became King of Judah only and eventually, King of all of Israel. David made mistakes and had many family problems but he always turned back to God in deep, genuine, heart-felt repentance

4. Example: Jesus: A great name by becoming of no reputation on earth –> Greatest name of all.

   a. Jesus was born in a manger. He submitted to His parents and learned carpentry before starting ministry. He became a traveling teacher with controversial teachings which got Him killed by religious leaders and governmental officials. He had twelve close followers who all abandoned Him in His time of greatest need.

   b. Matthew 11:29 - 29 Take my yoke upon you, and **learn from me, for I am gentle and lowly in heart**, and you will find rest for your souls.

   c. Philippians 2:7, 9 NKJV - 7 but **made Himself of no reputation**, taking the form of a bondservant, [and] coming in the likeness of men. ... 9 Therefore God also has highly exalted Him and **given Him the name which is above every name**,

   d. Isaiah 53:3 - 3 He was **despised and rejected by men**, a man of sorrows and acquainted with grief; and as one from whom men hide their faces he was despised, and **we esteemed him not**.

   e. John 1:10-11 - 10 He was in the world, and the world was made through him, **yet the world did not know him**. 11 He came to his own, and **his own people did not receive him**.

   f. 1 Peter 2:4 - 4 As you come to him, a living stone **rejected by men but in the sight of God chosen and precious**.

5. Advancing, building up, or protecting our own name and reputation is not the way to a great name in God's sight.

   a. Luke 6:22-23, 26 - 22 "**Blessed are you when people hate you and when they exclude you and revile you and spurn your name as evil, on account of the Son of Man!** 23 Rejoice in that day, and leap for joy, for behold, your reward is great in heaven; for so their fathers did to the prophets. ... 26 "**Woe to you, when all people speak well of you, for so their fathers did to the false prophets**.

   b. 1 John 4:5-6 - 5 **They are from the world**; therefore they speak from the world, and **the world listens to them**. 6 We are from God. **Whoever knows God listens to us; whoever is not from God does not listen to us**. By this we know the Spirit of truth and the spirit of error.

   c. John 5:43-44 - 43 I have come in my Father's name, and you do not receive me. If another comes in his own name, you will receive him. 44 **How can you believe, when you receive glory from one another and do not seek the glory that comes from the only God**?

C. Zealous for God's Glory

1. Seeking for God's glory is about allowing God to build His own reputation in His own way, in His own time, and through obedience to His instructions, even if it means the detriment of our own reputations, desires, and our very lives.

   > Glory: Hebrew-H3519: *kabod/kavod*: 1. Glory, honor. 2. Abundance, riches, splendor. 3. Dignity, reputation, reverence.

   a. The word "glory" is derived from the root word for weight or weightiness.
      i. To bring glory to God is to *give weight* to who He is, what He does, and what He commands.
      ii. To bring glory to God means to do things His way so that HIS reputation is built up and people *give weight* to who He is and what He does.
      iii. Example: God gained "weightiness" over Pharaoh in the sight of all nations through Israel's exodus from Egypt. (Exodus 14:4, 17-18.)
         01. God gained the reputation as being more powerful than Pharaoh, the most powerful man in the world.

   b. Being zealous for God's glory means being passionate about God making Himself known and showing Himself mighty.
      i. This is done through selfless obedience to His instructions, doing things His way, waiting for His timing, and letting Him be God so that HIS reputation is built.
      ii. This often means humbling ourselves to total childlike dependence so that God does the impossible on our behalf and truthfully deserves and receives all the credit.
         01. It does not mean showing off our own strengths, power, wisdom, or wealth and saying, "to God be the glory."
      iii. It does not mean forcing God on people or using God's name for behavior that is out of order and against God's ways.
      iv. It does not mean seeking a spiritual realm or creating an atmosphere.

   c. Being jealous for God's glory means guarding God's reputation as something precious so that He is esteemed.
      i. Obeying God and representing Him well so that others come to know Him and His character, mercy, love, and power.
      ii. Desiring for God's name to be represented properly and held in esteem.

   d. Example: God's glory through Gideon.
      i. God was going to gain glory for Himself by showing Himself mighty on Israel's behalf.
      ii. To do so, God raised up Gideon as a leader of the people against Israel's enemies.
      iii. Gideon assembled 32,000 men to fight against the enemies of Israel.
      iv. God would not allow them to fight with an army that large. He knew that Gideon and the army would take credit/glory for themselves and their own strength and military prowess.
         01. Judges 7:2 - 2 The LORD said to Gideon, "The people with you are too many for me to give the Midianites into their hand, **lest Israel boast over me, saying, 'My own hand has saved me.'**
         02. God continued to reduce the number of fighting men from 32,000 to 300.
      v. God's military command was to smash clay pots and blow trumpets. At this, HE would defeat the enemies of Israel. It was not done through human military strategy.

- 01. A simple, if not ridiculous, approach militarily demonstrated that the power was God's and not man's.
- 02. God gave the victory. God rightly deserves all the credit.
- 03. God's reputation was built in the sight of the nations because they were defeated by a small and silly military - who had the power of a great God.
- vi. Note: Gideon could not help but include himself and his reputation in the miliary shout.
    - 01. Judges 7:18 - 18 When I blow the trumpet, I and all who are with me, then blow the trumpets also on every side of all the camp and shout, **'For the LORD and for Gideon.'**"
    - 02. Gideon went on to be a violent and self-aggrandizing leader. He was not zealous or jealous for God's glory. He wanted glory and honor for Himself.

2. The purpose of God's blessing is to make Him known to all nations and give Him highest honor in the sight of all mankind.

    a. Psalm 67:1-7 - 1 May God be gracious to us and bless us and make his face to shine upon us, Selah 2 **that your way may be known on earth, your saving power among all nations.** 3 Let the peoples praise you, O God; let all the peoples praise you! 4 Let the nations be glad and sing for joy, for you judge the peoples with equity and guide the nations upon earth. Selah 5 Let the peoples praise you, O God; let all the peoples praise you! 6 The earth has yielded its increase; God, our God, shall bless us. 7 **God shall bless us; let all the ends of the earth fear him**!
    - i. The blessing of God upon His people is to build His reputation in all the earth.
    - ii. His aim is for all people in every nation to fear Him and know His salvation.

    b. Deuteronomy 4:5-8 - 5 See, I have taught you statutes and rules, as the LORD my God commanded me, that you should do them in the land that you are entering to take possession of it. 6 Keep them and do them, for **that will be your wisdom and your understanding in the sight of the peoples, who, when they hear all these statutes, will say, 'Surely this great nation is a wise and understanding people.'** 7 **For what great nation is there that has a god so near to it as the LORD our God is to us, whenever we call upon him?** 8 And **what great nation is there, that has statutes and rules so righteous as all this law** that I set before you today?
    - i. Observing God's commands and obeying His instructions reveals God's wisdom and justice to the rest of the world.
    - ii. Calling upon the Lord for help reveals to the world God's nearness, goodness, and power towards His people.

3. Examples of people who knew the purpose of God being glorified:

    a. David defeating Goliath so that all the earth could hear of the God of Israel and that Israel would know that God saves without a sword.
    - i. 1 Samuel 17:45-47 - 45 Then David said to the Philistine, "You come to me with a sword and with a spear and with a javelin, but I come to you in the name of the LORD of hosts, the God of the armies of Israel, whom you have defied. 46 This day the LORD will deliver you into my hand, and I will strike you down and cut off your head. And I will give the dead bodies of the host of the Philistines this day to the birds of the air and to the wild beasts of the earth, **that all the earth may know that there is a God in Israel**, 47 **and that all this assembly may know that the LORD saves not with sword and spear**. For the battle is the LORD's, and he will give you into our hand."
        - 01. Note: David was not motivated by the earthly reward or bounty offered to the Israelite who could defeat the Philistine.

- b. David thanking God for granting him an eternal kingdom and great name so that God's name would be great in all the earth.
    - i. 2 Samuel 7:23-26 - 23 And who is like your people Israel, the one nation on earth whom God went to redeem to be his people, **making himself a name** and doing for them great and awesome things by driving out before your people, whom you redeemed for yourself from Egypt, a nation and its gods? 24 And you established for yourself your people Israel to be your people forever. And you, O LORD, became their God. 25 And now, O LORD God, confirm forever the word that you have spoken concerning your servant and concerning his house, and do as you have spoken. 26 **And your name will be magnified forever, saying, 'The LORD of hosts is God over Israel,'** and the house of your servant David will be established before you.
        - 01. Even when God blessed David with a covenant of an eternal dynasty, David knew that everything God did for Israel was for God to make a name for Himself.

- c. Solomon's dedication of the Temple so that all nations would know the God of Israel.
    - i. 1 Kings 8:59-60 - 59 Let these words of mine, with which I have pleaded before the LORD, be near to the LORD our God day and night, and may he maintain the cause of his servant and the cause of his people Israel, as each day requires, 60 **that all the peoples of the earth may know that the LORD is God; there is no other.**
        - 01. The purpose of the Temple is for God to dwell with His people, to glorify God, and to give all people everywhere the opportunity to seek Him and know Him.
        - 02. This gives an indication as to why it is so offensive to turn God's House into a marketplace charging money from people rather than place of prayer for people from all nations to come to know God.

- d. Elijah's prayer for fire from heaven to stop the people from limping between two opinions so that they would know for certain that the Lord is God.
    - i. 1 Kings 18:36-37 - 36 And at the time of the offering of the oblation, Elijah the prophet came near and said, "O LORD, God of Abraham, Isaac, and Israel, **let it be known this day that you are God in Israel, and that I am your servant**, and that I have done all these things at your word. 37 Answer me, O LORD, answer me, **that this people may know that you, O LORD, are God**, and that you have turned their hearts back."
        - 01. Elijah only wanted God to magnify Himself as more powerful than Baal so that the people's hearts would turn back to God.
        - 02. Elijah was not motivated by putting on a fire show for his own reputation.

- e. Hezekiah's prayer for help against the Assyrians (who had already demolished all the surrounding nations) so that all the nations would know that the God of Israel reigns.
    - i. 2 Kings 19:17-19 - 17 Truly, O LORD, the kings of Assyria have laid waste the nations and their lands 18 and have cast their gods into the fire, for they were not gods, but the work of men's hands, wood and stone. Therefore they were destroyed. 19 So now, O LORD our God, save us, please, from his hand, **that all the kingdoms of the earth may know that you, O LORD, are God alone.**"
        - 01. Hezekiah wanted God to show Himself more powerful than Assyria, who had already conquered many kingdoms, including the northern kingdom, Israel.

4. Jesus' teaching, prayer, obedience, and the cross, were all for God to be glorified.

a. John 7:16-18 - 16 So Jesus answered them, "My teaching is not mine, but his who sent me. 17 If anyone's will is to do God's will, he will know whether the teaching is from God or whether I am speaking on my own authority. 18 **The one who speaks on his own authority seeks his own glory; but the one who seeks the glory of him who sent him is true, and in him there is no falsehood.**
    i. Jesus was not trying to build His own reputation or following.
    ii. His entire purpose was to deliver the message of God and build God's reputation.

b. John 12:27-28 - 27 "Now is my soul troubled. And what shall I say? 'Father, save me from this hour'? But for this purpose I have come to this hour. 28 **Father, glorify your name.**" Then a voice came from heaven: "I have glorified it, and I will glorify it again."
    i. As He prepared for the cross, Jesus knew it would be for the glory of God - to build God's reputation as the Most High in all the earth, sovereign over life and death.

c. John 13:31-32 - 31 When he [Judas] had gone out [to betray Him], Jesus said, "Now is the Son of Man glorified, and **God is glorified in him.** 32 If **God is glorified in him, God will also glorify him in himself**, and glorify him at once.
    i. This was immediately following Judas leaving the room to betray Him.
    ii. Jesus knew that after His betrayal, suffering, and death, God would be greatly honored through demonstration of resurrection power and sovereignty over death.

d. John 17:1-3 - 1 When Jesus had spoken these words, he lifted up his eyes to heaven, and said, "Father, the hour has come; **glorify your Son that the Son may glorify you**, 2 since you have given him authority over all flesh, to give eternal life to all whom you have given him. 3 And this is eternal life, **that they know you, the only true God, and Jesus Christ whom you have sent**.
    i. In His final prayer before His arrest, Jesus offered Himself over to death so that God's reputation could be established and proclaimed in all the earth.
    ii. Jesus gave Himself over to total childlike dependence on God so that God could do the impossible and receive all the credit.

Unit Two: The Way to Destruction: Pride & Selfish Ambition

> Everyone who is arrogant in heart is an abomination to the LORD; be assured, he will not go unpunished.
>
> Proverbs 16:5

A. Arrogance

1. Arrogance is an abomination in God's sight.

    a. Proverbs 6:16-19 - 16 There are six things that the LORD hates, seven that are an **abomination to him**: 17 **haughty eyes**, a lying tongue, and hands that shed innocent blood, 18 a heart that devises wicked plans, feet that make haste to run to evil, 19 a false witness who breathes out lies, and one who sows discord among brothers.

        > Haughty/Proud: Hebrew-H7311: *rum*: 1. To lift oneself up. To rise. To show oneself powerful. 2. To rise up or be exalted. 3. To raise, lift up, set up, erect, exalt, set on high. 4. To exalt oneself or magnify oneself. 5. To be rotten or wormy.

    b. Proverbs 16:5 - 5 **Everyone who is arrogant in heart is an abomination to the LORD**; be assured, he will not go unpunished.

    c. Psalm 101:5 - 5 Whoever slanders his neighbor secretly I will destroy. **Whoever has a haughty look and an arrogant heart I will not endure.**

    d. Habakkuk 2:4 - 4 Behold, **his soul is puffed up; it is not upright within him**, but the righteous shall live by his faith.

        > Puffed Up: Hebrew-H6075: *apal*: 1. To lift up, swell, or be lifted up. 2. To presume or be heedless.

2. Arrogance is self-willed, self-sufficiency and doing things in your own strength. It is denying God and your need for Him.

    > Arrogant: Greek-G829: *authades*: 1. Self-pleasing. 2. Self-willed. 3. Arrogant. Root words: Self. Pleasure.

    a. Example: No fear of the Lord, self-flattery, plotting self-advancement, failure to reject evil.
        i. Psalm 36:1-4 - 1 **Transgression** speaks to the wicked deep in his heart; **there is no fear of God** before his eyes. 2 For **he flatters himself in his own eyes** that his iniquity cannot be found out and hated. 3 The words of his mouth are trouble and deceit; he has **ceased to act wisely and do good**. 4 He **plots trouble** while on his bed; he **sets himself in a way that is not good; he does not reject evil.**
            01. Psalm 36:2 NIV - In their own eyes they **flatter themselves too much to detect or hate their sin.**
            02. Without the fear of the Lord, there is no wisdom. This results in evil.

b. Example: Nimrod & Babel.
   i. Genesis 10:8-12 - 8 Cush fathered **Nimrod; he was the first on earth to be a mighty man**. 9 **He was a mighty hunter before the LORD**. Therefore it is said, "Like Nimrod a mighty hunter before the LORD." 10 **The beginning of his kingdom was Babel**, Erech, Accad, and Calneh, in the land of Shinar. 11 From that land he went into Assyria and built Nineveh, Rehoboth-Ir, Calah, and 12 Resen between Nineveh and Calah; that is the great city.
      01. Nimrod was a man of great strength and hunting prowess. He used his strength to overpower people and to build cities to store up the spoils of his hunting and the treasure he plundered from others.
   ii. Genesis 11:3-4 - 3 And they said to one another, "Come, let us make bricks, and burn them thoroughly." And they had brick for stone, and bitumen for mortar. 4 Then they said, "**Come, let us build ourselves a city and a tower with its top in the heavens, and let us make a name for ourselves**, lest we be dispersed over the face of the whole earth."
      01. Nimrod gathered all the people of the world together to build a tower with the latest technology in that day: the brick. The goal was to reach the heavens on their own to make a name for themselves rather than exalting the Lord or relying on Him to come down to them and to avert His judgment of scattering them.

c. Example: Lighting your own way by your own devices or living by the light of God.
   i. Isaiah 50:10-11 - 10 Who among you fears the LORD and obeys the voice of his servant? **Let him who walks in darkness and has no light trust in the name of the LORD and rely on his God**. 11 Behold, all you who kindle a fire, **who equip yourselves with burning torches! Walk by the light of your fire, and by the torches that you have kindled! This you have from my hand: you shall lie down in torment**.

d. Example: Determining your own outcome and pursuing it in your own strength instead of Inquiring of the Lord in all situations.
   i. Isaiah 9:8-13 - 8 The Lord has sent a word against Jacob, and it will fall on Israel; 9 and all the people will know, Ephraim and the inhabitants of Samaria, who say in pride and in arrogance of heart: 10 "**The bricks have fallen, but we will build with dressed stones; the sycamores have been cut down, but we will put cedars in their place**." 11 But the LORD raises the adversaries of Rezin against him, and stirs up his enemies. 12 The Syrians on the east and the Philistines on the west devour Israel with open mouth. For all this his anger has not turned away, and his hand is stretched out still. 13 **The people did not turn to him who struck them, nor inquire of the LORD of hosts**.

3. Mankind in its natural state does not glorify God and does not want to honor Him. God's wrath is to turn people over to their own arrogance.

   a. Romans 1:18-32 - 18 For the wrath of God is revealed from heaven against all ungodliness and unrighteousness of men, who **by their unrighteousness suppress the truth**. 19 For what can be known about God is plain to them, because God has shown it to them. 20 For his invisible attributes, namely, his eternal power and divine nature, have been clearly perceived, ever since the creation of the world, in the things that have been made. So they are without excuse. 21 For **although they knew God, they did not honor him as God or give thanks to him, but they became futile in their thinking**, and their foolish hearts were darkened. 22 Claiming to be wise, they became fools, 23 and **exchanged the glory of the immortal God for images** resembling mortal man and birds and animals and creeping things. 24 Therefore God gave them up in the lusts of their hearts to impurity, to the dishonoring of their bodies among themselves, 25 because they **exchanged the truth about God for a lie and worshiped and served the creature rather than the Creator**, who is blessed forever! Amen. 26 For this reason God gave them up to dishonorable passions. For their women exchanged natural relations for those that are contrary to nature; 27 and the men likewise gave up natural relations with women and were consumed with passion for one another, men committing shameless acts with men and receiving in themselves the due penalty for their error. 28 And since **they did not see fit to acknowledge God**, God gave them up to a debased mind to do what ought not to be done. 29 They were filled with all manner of unrighteousness, evil, covetousness, malice. They are full of envy, murder, strife, deceit, maliciousness. They are gossips, 30 slanderers, **haters of God, insolent, haughty, boastful,** inventors of evil, disobedient to parents, 31 foolish, faithless, heartless, ruthless. 32 **Though they know God's righteous decree that those who practice such things deserve to die, they not only do them but give approval to those who practice them.**

B. Self-Praise, Glory, & Boasting

1. Self-praise and receiving praise from others.

    a. Proverbs 27:2 - **2 Let another praise you, and not your own mouth**; a stranger, and **not your own lips**.

    b. Proverbs 25:27 - 27 It is not good to eat much honey, **nor is it glorious to seek one's own glory**.

    c. Proverbs 30:32-33 - 32 **If you have been foolish, exalting yourself**, or if you have been devising evil, **put your hand on your mouth**. 33 For pressing milk produces curds, pressing the nose produces blood, and pressing anger produces strife.

2. Receiving praise and seeking glory from man.

    a. Proverbs 27:21 NLT - 21 Fire tests the purity of silver and gold, but **a person is tested by being praised**.

    b. Example: Herod Antipas received glory from man and did not give glory to God.
        i. Acts 12:20-23 - 20 Now Herod was angry with the people of Tyre and Sidon, and they came to him with one accord, and having persuaded Blastus, the king's chamberlain, they asked for peace, because their country depended on the king's country for food. 21 On an appointed day Herod put on his royal robes, took his seat upon the throne, and delivered an oration to them. 22 **And the people were shouting, "The voice of a god, and not of a man!" 23 Immediately an angel of the Lord struck him down, because he did not give God the glory, and he was eaten by worms and breathed his last.**

    c. Example: Pharisees sought glory from man rather than God and exalted themselves.
        i. Matthew 23:5-7, 11-12 - 5 **They do all their deeds to be seen by others**. For they make their phylacteries broad and their fringes long, 6 and **they love the place of honor at feasts and the best seats in the synagogues** 7 and greetings in the marketplaces and being called rabbi by others. ... 11 The greatest among you shall be your servant. 12 **Whoever exalts himself** will be humbled, and whoever humbles himself will be exalted.
        ii. Luke 14:7, 11 - 7 Now he told a parable to those who were invited, **when he noticed how they chose the places of honor**, saying to them, ... 11 For **everyone who exalts himself** will be humbled, and he who humbles himself will be exalted."

  iii. John 5:44 - 44 How can you believe, **when you receive glory from one another** and do not seek the glory that comes from the only God?

3. Boasting. Self-satisfied talk of one's own accomplishments, possessions, abilities, or endeavors.

 a. Example: The king of Assyria boasted that his own strength and military might had allowed him to conquer the lands of many peoples, including Israel. But it was the Lord who gave him the right and ability to conquer these people – he was nothing but an axe of judgment in the hand of God being used by God for His sovereign purposes in the earth.
  i. Isaiah 10:13-19 - 13 **For he says: "By the strength of my hand I have done it**, and **by my wisdom**, for I have understanding; **I remove the boundaries of peoples**, and plunder their treasures; **like a bull I bring down those who sit on thrones**. 14 **My hand** has found like a nest the wealth of the peoples; and as one gathers eggs that have been forsaken, so **I have gathered all the earth**; and there was none that moved a wing or opened the mouth or chirped." 15 **Shall the axe boast over him who hews with it, or the saw magnify itself against him who wields it? As if a rod should wield him who lifts it, or as if a staff should lift him who is not wood!**

 b. Boasting about tomorrow and your own plans.
  i. James 4:13-16 - 13 Come now, **you who say, "Today or tomorrow we will go into such and such a town and spend a year there and trade and make a profit"**-- 14 yet you do not know what tomorrow will bring. What is your life? For you are a mist that appears for a little time and then vanishes. 15 **Instead you ought to say, "If the Lord wills, we will live and do this or that."** 16 As it is, **you boast in your arrogance. All such boasting is evil.**
  ii. Proverbs 27:1 - 1 **Do not boast about tomorrow**, for you do not know what a day may bring.

 c. Example: False Apostles/Teachers boast in appearances, flesh, work in other's territory.
  i. 2 Corinthians 5:12 - 12 We are not commending ourselves to you again but giving you cause to boast about us, so that you may be able to answer **those who boast about outward appearance** and not about what is in the heart.
   01. For example: how many followers they have, how many people come to their meetings, what great things they have been doing, etc.
  ii. 2 Corinthians 11:18, 22 - 18 **Since many boast according to the flesh**, I too will boast. ... 22 Are they Hebrews? So am I. Are they Israelites? So am I. Are they offspring of Abraham? So am I.
   01. For example: any natural ability, aspect, or seeming advantage in their service to the Lord.
  iii. 2 Corinthians 10:16 - 16 so that we may preach the gospel in lands beyond you, without **boasting of work already done in another's area of influence.**
   01. For example: enjoying the ease of ministering in an area that has been evangelized without having done the hard work of breaking ground.

 d. In contrast to false teachers, Paul refused to boast (even though he could have done so truthfully) in order to not create an impression of himself in people's minds other than what they experienced of him for themselves.
  i. 2 Corinthians 12:6 - 6 though if I should wish to boast, I would not be a fool, for I would be speaking the truth; but **I refrain from it, so that no one may think more of me than he sees in me or hears from me.**

- e. Boasting only in the Lord.
    - i. Jeremiah 9:23-24 - 23 Thus says the LORD: "Let not the wise man boast in his wisdom, let not the mighty man boast in his might, let not the rich man boast in his riches, 24 **but let him who boasts boast in this, that he understands and knows me**, that I am the LORD who practices steadfast love, justice, and righteousness in the earth. For in these things I delight, declares the LORD."
    - ii. Galatians 6:14 - 14 But **far be it from me to boast except in the cross of our Lord Jesus Christ**, by which the world has been crucified to me, and I to the world.
    - iii. Ephesians 2:8-9 - 8 For by grace you have been saved through faith. And this is not your own doing; it is the gift of God, 9 not a result of works, **so that no one may boast**.
    - iv. 2 Corinthians 10:17-18 - 17 "**Let the one who boasts, boast in the Lord.**" 18 **For it is not the one who commends himself who is approved, but the one whom the Lord commends**.

C. Selfish Ambition

1. Selfish ambition is the root of man's first sin. It is the way of the world.

    a. Genesis 3:5 - 5 For God knows that when you eat of it your eyes will be opened, and **you will be like God**, knowing good and evil."
        - i. The serpent's deception was to provoke the woman to exalt herself to be like God.

    b. Genesis 3:6 - 6 So when the woman saw that the tree was good for food, and that it was a delight to the eyes, and that the tree was to be **desired to make one wise**, she took of its fruit and ate, and she also gave some to her husband who was with her, and he ate.
        - i. The forbidden fruit was desirable for her body, her eyes, and her self-advancement. Eve saw that eating the forbidden fruit would cause her to excel and have special knowledge which would empower her to advance herself.
        - ii. The word for wise is the same word for prosper. The same word in Deuteronomy 29:9 and Joshua 1:7 used to say that obeying God's commands will cause you to prosper.

    c. 1 John 2:16-17 - 16 For all that is in the world--the **desires of the flesh and the desires of the eyes and pride of life**--is not from the Father but **is from the world**. 17 And the world is passing away along with its desires, but whoever does the will of God abides forever.
        - i. Pursuing our own (unsanctified) desires is the opposite of doing the will of God.
        - ii. Pride of life includes boasting or confidence in empty assurances and false measures of success (i.e. wealth, fame, etc.) rather than God's measure of success.
            - 01. If your measurement of success when used to measure the life of Jesus causes Jesus to be a failure, you have the wrong measuring tool.
            - 02. God's measure of success is weighed by purity of heart and faithfulness.

2. Selfish ambition is evil. Posturing for your own advancement, protection, provision, and position causes strife, conflict, and superiority - things God hates.

    a. Proverbs 21:4 KJV - 4 An **high look**, and a **proud heart**, and the **plowing of the wicked**, is sin.
        - i. <u>A high look</u>: Looking down on other people.
            - 01. Example: Pharisee looking down on tax collector.
        - ii. <u>A proud heart</u>: the word translated as proud here actually means large, at liberty, wide, or broad. Therefore, the meaning could be seen as "having big plans."
            - 01. Example: Nimrod & Babel.

iii. <u>The plowing of the wicked</u>: is also translated as lamp. A heart like soil without the seed of God, working/burning towards its own devices.

b. James 3:14-16 - 14 **But if you have bitter jealousy and selfish ambition in your hearts, do not boast and be false to the truth.** 15 This is not the wisdom that comes down from above, but is earthly, unspiritual, demonic. 16 For **where jealousy and selfish ambition exist, there will be disorder and every vile practice**.

> <u>Selfish Ambition</u>: Greek-G2052: *eritheia*: 1. Electioneering or intriguing for office. 2. A desire to put oneself forward, a partisan and fractious spirit which does not disdain low arts. 3. To spin wool. 4. Self-seeking.
>
> <u>Jealousy</u>: Greek-G2205: *zelos*: 1. Zeal. 2. Envying. 3. Indignation. 4. Excitement of mind, ardor, fervor of spirit. 5. Envious and contentious rivalry.

c. James 4:1-4 - 1 **What causes quarrels and what causes fights among you? Is it not this, that your passions are at war within you?** 2 You desire and do not have, so you murder. **You covet and cannot obtain, so you fight and quarrel.** You do not have, because you do not ask. 3 You ask and do not receive, because you ask wrongly, to spend it on your passions. 4 **You adulterous people! Do you not know that friendship with the world is enmity with God?** Therefore whoever wishes to be a friend of the world makes himself an enemy of God.
   i. Selfish ambition causes anger, quarrels, and fights between people.
   ii. Selfish ambition is the way of the world and makes us enemies of God.

3. Example: Jesus' disciples argued over who was the greatest and postured for position.

   a. Luke 9:46-48 - 46 **An argument arose among them as to which of them was the greatest.** 47 But Jesus, knowing the reasoning of their hearts, took a child and put him by his side 48 and said to them, "Whoever receives this child in my name receives me, and whoever receives me receives him who sent me. For he who is least among you all is the one who is great."
      i. Jesus' disciples exalted themselves. Jesus exalted a child.

   b. Mark 10:35-41 - 35 And **James and John, the sons of Zebedee, came up to him and said to him, "Teacher, we want you to do for us whatever we ask of you."** 36 And he said to them, "What do you want me to do for you?" 37 And they said to him, **"Grant us to sit, one at your right hand and one at your left, in your glory."** 38 Jesus said to them, "You do not know what you are asking. Are you able to drink the cup that I drink, or to be baptized with the baptism with which I am baptized?" 39 And they said to him, "We are able." And Jesus said to them, "The cup that I drink you will drink, and with the baptism with which I am baptized, you will be baptized, 40 but to sit at my right hand or at my left is not mine to grant, but it is for those for whom it has been prepared." 41 **And when the ten heard it, they began to be indignant at James and John.**
      i. Without them understanding what He meant, Jesus clearly told them the way to greatness was through giving their lives for God and His Kingdom.

4. Example: The Corinthian believers were full of strife and divisions because they were following and taking pride in teachers whose ministries they liked and wanted to be known affiliates of.

   a. 1 Corinthians 3:1-4 - 1 But I, brothers, could not address you as spiritual people, but as people of the flesh, as infants in Christ. 2 I fed you with milk, not solid food, for you were not ready for it. And even now you are not yet ready, 3 for you are still of the flesh. **For while there is jealousy**

and strife among you, are you not of the flesh and behaving only in a human way? 4 For when one says, "I follow Paul," and another, "I follow Apollos," are you not being merely human?
- i. Positioning for superiority based on human leaders is carnal and worldly. (Paul calls it beastly, controlled by animal appetites.) We all have one leader: His name is Jesus.

5. Example: Korah assembled men in rebellion against Moses, accusing Moses of exalting himself over them. Out of selfish ambition, they wanted Moses and Aaron's positions for themselves and were willing to put themselves forward in force in order to obtain it.

    a. Numbers 16:1-3 - 1 **Now Korah** the son of Izhar, son of Kohath, son of Levi, and Dathan and Abiram the sons of Eliab, and On the son of Peleth, sons of Reuben, **took men**. 2 **And they rose up before Moses, with a number of the people of Israel, 250 chiefs of the congregation, chosen from the assembly, well-known men**. 3 **They assembled themselves together against Moses and against Aaron** and said to them, "You have gone too far! For all in the congregation are holy, every one of them, and the LORD is among them. **Why then do you exalt yourselves above the assembly of the LORD?**"
        - i. Korah electioneered to gather people together under his leadership in opposition to Moses' leadership.
        - ii. Note: They were exalting themselves but accused Moses of exalting himself.

    b. Numbers 16:8-11 - 8 And Moses said to Korah, "Hear now, you sons of Levi: 9 **is it too small a thing for you that the God of Israel has separated you from the congregation of Israel, to bring you near to himself, to do service in the tabernacle of the LORD and to stand before the congregation to minister to them**, 10 and that he has brought you near him, and all your brothers the sons of Levi with you? **And would you seek the priesthood also?** 11 Therefore it is against the LORD that you and all your company have gathered together. What is Aaron that you grumble against him?"
        - i. Korah and the Levites had already been specially selected by God to minister in the tabernacle but they wanted more. What God had given them was not enough for them, they wanted the top position of authority - to be like God.

    c. Numbers 16:12-14 - 12 And Moses sent to call Dathan and Abiram the sons of Eliab, and they said, "We will not come up. 13 **Is it a small thing that you have brought us up out of a land flowing with milk and honey, to kill us in the wilderness, that you must also make yourself a prince over us?** 14 Moreover, **you have not brought us into a land flowing with milk and honey, nor given us inheritance of fields and vineyards**. Will you put out the eyes of these men? We will not come up."
        - i. Korah and his company stubbornly refused to heed the instructions of Moses.
        - ii. Their perspective had become so distorted that they called Egypt the land of milk and honey and raged against Moses for not bringing them into the Promised Land.

    d. Numbers 16:24, 32-33 - 24 "Say to the congregation, Get away from the dwelling of Korah, Dathan, and Abiram." ... 32 **And the earth opened its mouth and swallowed them up, with their households and all the people who belonged to Korah and all their goods. 33 So they and all that belonged to them went down alive into Sheol, and the earth closed over them, and they perished from the midst of the assembly**.
        - i. God separated the non-rebels from the ambitious and the earth swallowed them up.

6. Example: David's son Absalom wanted to be king. He campaigned for the hearts of the people by promising them justice. Once he had the hearts of the people, he declared himself to be king with such a large group that even David, the mighty warrior, fled the city for safety.

a. 2 Samuel 15:1-6 - 1 After this Absalom got himself a chariot and horses, and fifty men to run before him. 2 **And Absalom used to rise early and stand beside the way of the gate. And when any man had a dispute to come before the king for judgment**, Absalom would call to him and say, "From what city are you?" And when he said, "Your servant is of such and such a tribe in Israel," 3 **Absalom would say to him, "See, your claims are good and right, but there is no man designated by the king to hear you." 4 Then Absalom would say, "Oh that I were judge in the land! Then every man with a dispute or cause might come to me, and I would give him justice.**" 5 And whenever a man came near to pay homage to him, he would put out his hand and take hold of him and kiss him. 6 **Thus Absalom did to all of Israel who came to the king for judgment. So Absalom stole the hearts of the men of Israel**.
    i. Absalom electioneered among the people by intercepting communications and pleas for justice that were intended for the king in order to position himself in the hearts of the people.

b. 2 Samuel 15:10-14 - 10 But Absalom sent secret messengers throughout all the tribes of Israel, saying, "**As soon as you hear the sound of the trumpet, then say, 'Absalom is king at Hebron!'**" 11 With Absalom went two hundred men from Jerusalem who were invited guests, and they went in their innocence and knew nothing. 12 And while Absalom was offering the sacrifices, he sent for Ahithophel the Gilonite, David's counselor, from his city Giloh. And the conspiracy grew strong, and the people with Absalom kept increasing. 13 **And a messenger came to David, saying, "The hearts of the men of Israel have gone after Absalom**." 14 Then David said to all his servants who were with him at Jerusalem, "Arise, and let us flee, or else there will be no escape for us from Absalom. Go quickly, lest he overtake us quickly and bring down ruin on us and strike the city with the edge of the sword."
    i. Through deception and intrigue, Absalom exalted himself to a position only God can ordain. He manipulated the hearts of the people to exalt him over David.

c. 2 Samuel 16:20-23 - 20 Then Absalom said to Ahithophel, "Give your counsel. What shall we do?" 21 Ahithophel said to Absalom, "**Go in to your father's concubines, whom he has left to keep the house, and all Israel will hear that you have made yourself a stench to your father, and the hands of all who are with you will be strengthened**." 22 So they pitched a tent for Absalom on the roof. **And Absalom went in to his father's concubines in the sight of all Israel**. 23 Now in those days the counsel that Ahithophel gave was as if one consulted the word of God; so was all the counsel of Ahithophel esteemed, both by David and by Absalom.
    i. Absalom took counsel for the exaltation of himself in triumph over David in the sight of all the peoples.

d. Absalom took great pride in his hair. (2 Samuel 14:25-26.) In his death, he died by his glorious hair getting caught in a tree as he rode under it on a horse. He was hanged by the hair he took such pride in. (2 Samuel 18:9.)

7. Example: David's son Adonijah wanted to be king instead of Solomon, so he put himself forward.

    a. 1 Kings 1:5 - 5 Now Adonijah the son of Haggith **exalted himself, saying, "I will be king."** And he prepared for himself chariots and horsemen, and fifty men to run before him.

    b. 1 Kings 1:7-10 - 7 He conferred with Joab the son of Zeruiah and with Abiathar the priest. And they followed Adonijah and helped him. 8 But Zadok the priest and Benaiah the son of Jehoiada and Nathan the prophet and Shimei and Rei and David's mighty men were not with Adonijah. 9 Adonijah sacrificed sheep, oxen, and fattened cattle by the Serpent's Stone, which is beside En-rogel, and **he invited all his brothers, the king's sons, and all the**

royal officials of Judah, 10 but he did not invite Nathan the prophet or Benaiah or the mighty men or Solomon his brother.

   i. Adonijah conspired with other officials who would be on his side and threw a royal feast in his own honor. He failed to invite anyone who would oppose him by standing with David's appointment of Solomon as king.

   c. When David's response was to publicly proclaim Solomon as king, Adonijah's guests trembled with fear and Adonijah humbled himself at the horns of the altar. Solomon showed him mercy by letting him live in spite of his treason.

   d. Next, Adonijah also manipulated Bathsheba into trying to persuade Solomon to grant him David's concubines which would have been a royal acknowledgement. For this scheme, Solomon had him put to death.

   i. 1 Kings 2:24-25 - 24 Now therefore as the LORD lives, who has established me and placed me on the throne of David my father, and who has made me a house, as he promised, **Adonijah shall be put to death today**." 25 So King Solomon sent Benaiah the son of Jehoiada, and he struck him down, and he died.

8. Example: King of Babylon (& Lucifer) out of selfish ambition exalted themselves against God in an attempt to become their own god or like God. Isaiah says this is a taunt against the king of Babylon but it also includes the name Lucifer which indicates that it is also telling the story of the fall of Lucifer/Satan from heaven due to selfish ambition.

   a. Isaiah 14:12-17 - 12 "How you are fallen from heaven, O Day Star [Lucifer], son of Dawn! How you are cut down to the ground, you who laid the nations low! 13 **You said in your heart, 'I will ascend** to heaven; above the stars of God **I will set my throne on high; I will sit on the mount** of assembly in the far reaches of the north; 14 **I will ascend** above the heights of the clouds; **I will make myself like the Most High.**' 15 But you are brought down to Sheol, to the far reaches of the pit. 16 Those who see you will stare at you and ponder over you: 'Is this the man who made the earth tremble, who shook kingdoms, 17 who made the world like a desert and overthrew its cities, who did not let his prisoners go home?'

   i. Selfish ambition drove the evil one to exalt himself to be like God and take God's throne.
   ii. It also incited violence against others in the pursuit of self-advancement.

9. Example: False teachers are ambitious to gain many followers for themselves and be famous. Often, they teach things which disqualify people from salvation but don't care because their aim is their own success, not the success of the Gospel.

   a. Galatians 4:17 - 17 They make much of you, but for no good purpose. They want to shut you out, **that you may make much of them**.

   b. Philippians 1:15-18 - 15 Some indeed **preach Christ from envy and rivalry**, but others from good will. 16 The latter do it out of love, knowing that I am put here for the defense of the gospel. 17 The former **proclaim Christ out of selfish ambition, not sincerely** but thinking to afflict me in my imprisonment. 18 What then? Only that in every way, whether in pretense or in truth, Christ is proclaimed, and in that I rejoice. Yes, and I will rejoice,

D. The Love of Money

1. Example: Pharisees and religious people love money because they think it makes them appear successful. But it is an abomination in the sight of God.

    a. Luke 16:13-15 - 13 No servant can serve two masters, for either he will hate the one and love the other, or he will be devoted to the one and despise the other. You cannot serve God and money." 14 **The Pharisees, who were lovers of money, heard all these things, and they ridiculed him.** 15 And he said to them, "**You are those who justify yourselves before men**, but God knows your hearts. **For what is exalted among men is an abomination in the sight of God**.
        i. The things that the world boasts about are like dung in the sight of God. (i.e. Money, wealth, the best clothes, cars, house, neighborhood, praise of men, etc.)

2. Example: False teachers emphasize money because they are using the name of God for their own selfish gain. Their teaching fosters speculations which cause friction between people in order to stir up a name for themselves and gain a following.

    a. 1 Timothy 6:3-10 - 3 If anyone teaches a different doctrine and does not agree with the sound words of our Lord Jesus Christ and the teaching that accords with godliness, 4 **he is puffed up with conceit and understands nothing.** He has an unhealthy craving for controversy and for quarrels about words, which produce envy, dissension, slander, evil suspicions, 5 and constant friction among people who are **depraved in mind and deprived of the truth, imagining that godliness is a means of gain**. 6 But godliness with contentment is great gain, 7 for we brought nothing into the world, and we cannot take anything out of the world. 8 But if we have food and clothing, with these we will be content. 9 **But those who desire to be rich fall into temptation, into a snare, into many senseless and harmful desires that plunge people into ruin and destruction.** 10 **For the love of money is a root of all kinds of evils. It is through this craving that some have wandered away from the faith and pierced themselves with many pangs**.
        i. Teaching that does not pursue the aim of Christlike love and godliness (moral excellence) is arrogant and ignorant.
        ii. Teaching that makes wealth the aim of Christianity is depraved deception.
        iii. The desire to be rich leads into a snare of ruin, destruction, evil, and wandering away from the true faith and hope in Christ.

    b. 2 Peter 2:3, 14-16 - 3 And **in their greed they will exploit you with false words**. Their condemn-nation from long ago is not idle, and their destruction is not asleep. ... 14 They have eyes full of adultery, insatiable for sin. They entice unsteady souls. **They have hearts trained in greed**. Accursed children! 15 Forsaking the right way, they have gone astray. **They have followed the way of Balaam, the son of Beor, who loved gain from wrongdoing**, 16 but was rebuked for his own transgression; a speechless donkey spoke with human voice and restrained the prophet's madness.
        i. They might distort the truth to get you to give them money.
        ii. They might speak the truth but from a wrong spirit and receive pay for their labor "for the Lord."

3. Example: Ananias and Sapphira lied about their giving to appear to be more generous.

    a. Acts 5:1-11 - 1 **But a man named Ananias, with his wife Sapphira, sold a piece of property**, 2 **and with his wife's knowledge he kept back for himself some of the proceeds and brought only a part of it and laid it at the apostles' feet**. 3 But Peter said, "Ananias, **why has Satan filled your heart to lie to the Holy Spirit and to keep back for yourself part of the proceeds of the**

land?** 4 While it remained unsold, did it not remain your own? And after it was sold, was it not at your disposal? Why is it that you have contrived this deed in your heart? You have not lied to man but to God.**" 5 When Ananias heard these words, he fell down and breathed his last. And great fear came upon all who heard of it. 6 The young men rose and wrapped him up and carried him out and buried him. 7 After an interval of about three hours his wife came in, not knowing what had happened. 8 And Peter said to her, "Tell me whether you sold the land for so much." And she said, "Yes, for so much." 9 But Peter said to her, "**How is it that you have agreed together to test the Spirit of the Lord?** Behold, the feet of those who have buried your husband are at the door, and they will carry you out." 10 Immediately she fell down at his feet and breathed her last. When the young men came in they found her dead, and they carried her out and buried her beside her husband. 11 And great fear came upon the whole church and upon all who heard of these things.
- i. Others were selling lands and giving everything to the apostles.
- ii. Ananias and Sapphira had the right to give whatever they wanted to give or not give from the proceeds of the sale of their house.
- iii. The sin is not the holding back but the lying about it.
- iv. They were pretending to be more generous than they actually were to receive glory from man in the sight of believers.

4. Example: Simon the sorcerer tried to pay money for the spiritual gift of laying hands for people to receive the Holy Spirit.

    a. Acts 8:9-13, 18-24 - 9 But **there was a man named Simon**, who had previously practiced magic in the city and amazed the people of Samaria, saying that he himself was somebody great. 10 They all paid attention to him, from the least to the greatest, saying, "This man is the power of God that is called Great." 11 And they paid attention to him because for a long time he had amazed them with his magic. 12 But when they believed Philip as he preached good news about the kingdom of God and the name of Jesus Christ, they were baptized, both men and women. 13 Even Simon himself believed, and after being baptized he continued with Philip. And seeing signs and great miracles performed, he was amazed. ... 18 **Now when Simon saw that the Spirit was given through the laying on of the apostles' hands, he offered them money**, 19 **saying, "Give me this power also, so that anyone on whom I lay my hands may receive the Holy Spirit."** 20 **But Peter said to him, "May your silver perish with you, because you thought you could obtain the gift of God with money! 21 You have neither part nor lot in this matter, for your heart is not right before God. 22 Repent, therefore, of this wickedness of yours, and pray to the Lord that, if possible, the intent of your heart may be forgiven you**. 23 **For I see that you are in the gall of bitterness and in the bond of iniquity**." 24 And Simon answered, "Pray for me to the Lord, that nothing of what you have said may come upon me."
    - i. The gall of bitterness is the same word used before to describe rebellion against God while convincing oneself that it is ok. (See Deuteronomy 29:18.)
    - ii. This is why paying money for church positions is called "Simony."

5. Example: Judas loved money. He was the treasurer of Jesus' ministry and used to help himself to the funds. He betrayed the author of life for thirty pieces of silver. Then when he realized he had done wrong, he tried to use money to reverse what he had done.

    a. John 12:4-6 - 4 But **Judas Iscariot**, one of his disciples (he who was about to betray him), said, 5 "Why was this ointment not sold for three hundred denarii and given to the poor?" 6 **He said this, not because he cared about the poor, but because he was a thief, and having charge of the moneybag he used to help himself to what was put into it.**

b. Matthew 26:14-16 - 14 Then [after Mary anointed Jesus with expensive perfume for burial] one of the twelve, whose name was **Judas Iscariot**, went to the chief priests 15 and said, **"What will you give me if I deliver him over to you?" And they paid him thirty pieces of silver.** 16 And from that moment he sought an opportunity to betray him.

c. Luke 22:3-6 - 3 Then **Satan entered into Judas called Iscariot**, who was of the number of the twelve. 4 He went away and conferred with the chief priests and officers how he might betray him to them. 5 And they were glad, and **agreed to give him money**. 6 So he consented and sought an opportunity to betray him to them in the absence of a crowd.

d. Matthew 27:3-5 - 3 Then when Judas, his betrayer, saw that Jesus was condemned, he changed his mind and **brought back the thirty pieces of silver to the chief priests and the elders, 4 saying, "I have sinned by betraying innocent blood**." They said, "What is that to us? See to it yourself." 5 And **throwing down the pieces of silver into the temple, he departed, and he went and hanged himself**.

Unit Three: God Humbles the Proud & Exalts the Humble

> The LORD lifts up the humble; he casts the wicked to the ground.
> Psalm 147:6

A. **God Humbles the Proud and Exalts the Humble**

1. Sample Scriptures:

    a. Psalm 75:1-10 - 1 We give thanks to you, O God; we give thanks, for your name is near. We recount your wondrous deeds. 2 "At the set time that I appoint I will judge with equity. 3 When the earth totters, and all its inhabitants, it is I who keep steady its pillars. Selah 4 **I say to the boastful, 'Do not boast,' and to the wicked, 'Do not lift up your horn**; 5 **do not lift up your horn on high, or speak with haughty neck.**'" 6 For not from the east or from the west and not from the wilderness comes lifting up, 7 but **it is God who executes judgment, putting down one and lifting up another.** 8 For in the hand of the LORD there is a cup with foaming wine, well mixed, and he pours out from it, and all the wicked of the earth shall drain it down to the dregs. 9 But I will declare it forever; I will sing praises to the God of Jacob. 10 **All the horns of the wicked I will cut off, but the horns of the righteous shall be lifted up**.

    b. Psalm 31:23-24 - 23 Love the LORD, all you his saints! **The LORD preserves the faithful but abundantly repays the one who acts in pride.** 24 Be strong, and let your heart take courage, all you who wait for the LORD!

    c. Proverbs 29:23 - 23 **One's pride will bring him low, but he who is lowly in spirit will obtain honor.**

    d. Proverbs 18:12 - 12 **Before destruction a man's heart is haughty, but humility comes before honor.**

    e. Psalm 18:27 - 27 For **you save a humble people**, but the **haughty eyes you bring down**.

    f. Psalm 147:6 - 6 **The LORD lifts up the humble; he casts the wicked to the ground.**

    g. Proverbs 3:34 - 34 **Toward the scorners he is scornful**, but **to the humble he gives favor**.

    h. Proverbs 11:2 - 2 **When pride comes, then comes disgrace, but with the humble is wisdom.**

2. Example: Hannah's prayer.

    a. 1 Samuel 2:1-10 - 1 And Hannah prayed and said, "My heart exults in the LORD; my horn is exalted in the LORD. My mouth derides my enemies, because I rejoice in your salvation. 2 "There is none holy like the LORD: for there is none besides you; there is no rock like our God. 3 **Talk no more so very proudly, let not arrogance come from your mouth; for the LORD is a God of knowledge, and by him actions are weighed. 4 The bows of the mighty are broken, but the feeble bind on strength**. 5 Those who were full have hired themselves out for bread, but those who were hungry have ceased to hunger. The barren has borne seven, but she who has many children is forlorn. 6 The LORD kills and brings to life; he brings down to Sheol and raises up. 7 **The LORD makes poor and makes rich; he brings low and he exalts**. 8 **He raises up the poor from the dust; he lifts the needy from the ash heap to make them sit with princes and inherit a seat of honor**. For the pillars of the earth are the LORD's, and on them he has set the world. 9 He will guard the feet of his faithful ones, but the wicked shall be cut off in darkness, **for not by might shall a man prevail. 10 The adversaries of the LORD shall be broken to pieces; against them he will thunder in heaven. The LORD will judge the ends of the earth; he will give strength to his king and exalt the horn of his anointed**."

B. Example: Pharaoh's Hardened Heart

1. Pharaoh demonstrated utter arrogance and self-exaltation. He thought he was a god and therefore, refused to repent and humble himself before the Lord. Even after many plagues and devastations to his people, Pharaoh refused to humble himself.

    a. Exodus 5:1-2 - 1 Afterward Moses and Aaron went and said to Pharaoh, "Thus says the LORD, the God of Israel, 'Let my people go, that they may hold a feast to me in the wilderness.'" 2 But Pharaoh said, "**Who is the LORD, that I should obey his voice and let Israel go? I do not know the LORD, and moreover, I will not let Israel go**."

    b. Exodus 10:3 - 3 So Moses and Aaron went in to Pharaoh and said to him, "Thus says the LORD, the God of the Hebrews, '**How long will you refuse to humble yourself before me?** Let my people go, that they may serve me.

2. Pharaoh demanded a sign from God to demonstrate power that he should submit himself to. God worked miracles through Aaron and Moses to demonstrate His power to Pharaoh. At first, the sorcerers of Egypt were able to replicate the signs of God. But soon, they could not and they acknowledged the power of God. But Pharaoh's stubbornness grew so great that he refused to listen to counsel from his advisers even after the whole land of Egypt had been ravaged by the signs of God.

    a. Exodus 7:8-13 - 8 Then the LORD said to Moses and Aaron, 9 "When Pharaoh says to you, '**Prove yourselves by working a miracle**,' then you shall say to Aaron, 'Take your staff and cast it down before Pharaoh, that it may become a serpent.'" 10 So Moses and Aaron went to Pharaoh and did just as the LORD commanded. Aaron cast down his staff before Pharaoh and his servants, and it became a serpent. 11 Then Pharaoh summoned the wise men and the sorcerers, and they, the magicians of Egypt, also did the same by their secret arts. 12 For each man cast down his staff, and they became serpents. But Aaron's staff swallowed up their staffs. 13 **Still Pharaoh's heart was hardened, and he would not listen to them**, as the LORD had said.
        i. Note: An evil and adulterous generation demands a sign. (Matthew 16:4.)
        ii. Note: People with hard hearts who demand signs will not believe even if God raised the dead. (Luke 16:31.)

    b. Exodus 8:16-19 - 16 Then the LORD said to Moses, "Say to Aaron, 'Stretch out your staff and strike the dust of the earth, so that it may become gnats in all the land of Egypt.'" 17 And they did so. Aaron stretched out his hand with his staff and struck the dust of the earth, and there were gnats on man and beast. All the dust of the earth became gnats in all the land of

Egypt. 18 **The magicians tried by their secret arts to produce gnats, but they could not**. So there were gnats on man and beast. 19 **Then the magicians said to Pharaoh, "This is the finger of God." But Pharaoh's heart was hardened, and he would not listen to them**, as the LORD had said.

    c. Exodus 9:14-17 - 14 For this time I will send all my plagues on you yourself, and on your servants and your people, **so that you may know that there is none like me in all the earth**. 15 For **by now I could have put out my hand and struck you and your people with pestilence, and you would have been cut off from the earth**. 16 **But for this purpose I have raised you up, to show you my power, so that my name may be proclaimed in all the earth**. 17 **You are still exalting yourself** against my people and will not let them go.
        i. God could have destroyed the whole land of Egypt but was giving Pharaoh time to repent and let God's people go.
        ii. Note: God sovereignly raised up Pharaoh for the very purpose of glorifying Himself.

    d. Exodus 10:7 - 7 Then Pharaoh's servants said to him, "How long shall this man be a snare to us? **Let the men go**, that they may serve the LORD their God. **Do you not yet understand that Egypt is ruined?**"
        i. Pharaoh refused to see the obvious destruction of his land and the power of God.

3. In between the calamities of plagues, Pharaoh returned to his normal state, just as hardened as he had been before.

    a. Exodus 8:15 - 15 But when **Pharaoh saw that there was a respite, he hardened his heart** and would not listen to them, as the LORD had said.

    b. Exodus 9:34-35 - 34 But when **Pharaoh saw that the rain and the hail and the thunder had ceased, he sinned yet again and hardened his heart**, he and his servants. 35 So the heart of Pharaoh was hardened, and he did not let the people of Israel go, just as the LORD had spoken through Moses.

4. Pharaoh tried to compromise with God and make his own terms for obedience.

    a. Exodus 8:25, 28 - 25 Then Pharaoh called Moses and Aaron and said, "**Go, sacrifice to your God within the land**." ... 28 So Pharaoh said, "**I will let you go to sacrifice to the LORD your God in the wilderness; only you must not go very far away. Plead for me**."
        i. Within the land rather than in the wilderness.
        ii. In the wilderness but not very far.
        iii. Note: "Plead for me" demonstrates wanting relief, not genuine repentance

    b. Exodus 10:8-11 - 8 So Moses and Aaron were brought back to Pharaoh. And he said to them, "Go, serve the LORD your God. **But which ones are to go?**" 9 Moses said, "We will go with our young and our old. We will go with our sons and daughters and with our flocks and herds, for we must hold a feast to the LORD." 10 But he said to them, "The LORD be with you, **if ever I let you and your little ones go! Look, you have some evil purpose in mind**. 11 **No! Go, the men among you**, and serve the LORD, for that is what you are asking." And they were driven out from Pharaoh's presence.
        i. Only the men.
        ii. Note: Accusing servants of God of evil intent.

c. Exodus 10:24 - 24 Then Pharaoh called Moses and said, "Go, serve the LORD; your little ones also may go with you; **only let your flocks and your herds remain behind**."
      i. All the people but not the flocks and herds.

5. Pharaoh wanted relief from the plagues but without genuine repentance before the Lord.

   a. Exodus 9:27-30 - 27 Then Pharaoh sent and called Moses and Aaron and said to them, "**This time I have sinned; the LORD is in the right, and I and my people are in the wrong. 28 Plead with the LORD, for there has been enough of God's thunder and hail**. I will let you go, and you shall stay no longer." 29 Moses said to him, "As soon as I have gone out of the city, I will stretch out my hands to the LORD. The thunder will cease, and there will be no more hail, **so that you may know that the earth is the LORD's**. 30 **But as for you and your servants, I know that you do not yet fear the LORD God**."
      i. Moses knew that he was putting on a show of contrition.

   b. Exodus 10:16-18 - 16 Then Pharaoh hastily called Moses and Aaron and said, "**I have sinned against the LORD your God, and against you. 17 Now therefore, forgive my sin, please, only this once, and plead with the LORD your God only to remove this death from me**." 18 So he went out from Pharaoh and pleaded with the LORD.

6. Pharaoh charged after God's people, relying on own strength to defy the will of the Lord.

   a. Exodus 14:4 - 4 And I will harden Pharaoh's heart, and he will pursue them, and **I will get glory over Pharaoh and all his host, and the Egyptians shall know that I am the LORD**."
      i. This is how God gained glory over Pharaoh and the world's most powerful army.

   b. Exodus 14:22-30 - 22 And the people of Israel went into the midst of the sea on dry ground, the waters being a wall to them on their right hand and on their left. 23 The **Egyptians pursued and went in after them into the midst of the sea, all Pharaoh's horses, his chariots, and his horsemen**. 24 And in the morning watch the LORD in the pillar of fire and of cloud looked down on the Egyptian forces and **threw the Egyptian forces into a panic**, 25 **clogging their chariot wheels so that they drove heavily**. And the Egyptians said, "Let us flee from before Israel, for the LORD fights for them against the Egyptians." 26 Then the LORD said to Moses, "**Stretch out your hand over the sea, that the water may come back upon the Egyptians, upon their chariots, and upon their horsemen**." 27 So Moses stretched out his hand over the sea, and the sea returned to its normal course when the morning appeared. **And as the Egyptians fled into it, the LORD threw the Egyptians into the midst of the sea**. 28 **The waters returned and covered the chariots and the horsemen; of all the host of Pharaoh that had followed them into the sea, not one of them remained**. 29 But the people of Israel walked on dry ground through the sea, the waters being a wall to them on their right hand and on their left. 30 Thus the LORD saved Israel that day from the hand of the Egyptians, and Israel saw the **Egyptians dead on the seashore**.

C. Example: Nebuchadnezzar, the Chopped Tree

1. Background: These events occurred after Nebuchadnezzar had acknowledged the Most High God as God due to Daniel's interpretation of a prior dream. (Daniel 2.) Daniel had made clear to him that his kingdom had been granted him by God who appoints all kings, and not his own strength, power, or wisdom.

a. After humbling himself, Nebuchadnezzar proceeded to erect a 90-foot statue for people all over the world to worship him.
      i. When Daniel's three friends refused to worship the statue, they were thrown in a fiery furnace and lived because God was with them.
      ii. Nebuchadnezzar witnessed this and again acknowledged God as the Most High.

   b. However, Nebuchadnezzar was still arrogant and regarded his success as his own doing based on his own strength, ability, military prowess, and cunning.

2. Next in Daniel 4, Nebuchadnezzar is making an announcement to everyone in his dominion, which was the largest empire in the world at the time. It is a later time, years later, and he has humbled himself to acknowledge and publicly declare that the Lord is God.

   a. Daniel 4:1-3 - 1 King Nebuchadnezzar to all peoples, nations, and languages, that dwell in all the earth: Peace be multiplied to you! 2 **It has seemed good to me to show the signs and wonders that the Most High God has done for me.** 3 How great are his signs, how mighty his wonders! His kingdom is an everlasting kingdom, and his dominion endures from generation to generation.

3. Nebuchadnezzar had a disturbing dream.

   a. Daniel 4:4-5, 10-17 - 4 **I, Nebuchadnezzar, was at ease in my house and prospering in my palace.** 5 **I saw a dream that made me afraid.** As I lay in bed the fancies and the visions of my head alarmed me. ... 10 The visions of my head as I lay in bed were these: I saw, and behold, **a tree in the midst of the earth, and its height was great.** 11 **The tree grew and became strong, and its top reached to heaven, and it was visible to the end of the whole earth.** 12 Its leaves were beautiful and its fruit abundant, and in it was food for all. The beasts of the field found shade under it, and the birds of the heavens lived in its branches, and all flesh was fed from it. 13 "I saw in the visions of my head as I lay in bed, and behold, a watcher, a holy one, came down from heaven. 14 He proclaimed aloud and said thus: '**Chop down the tree and lop off its branches, strip off its leaves and scatter its fruit. Let the beasts flee from under it and the birds from its branches.** 15 **But leave the stump of its roots in the earth, bound with a band of iron and bronze, amid the tender grass of the field.** Let him be wet with the dew of heaven. Let his portion be with the beasts in the grass of the earth. 16 Let his mind be changed from a man's, and let a beast's mind be given to him; and let seven periods of time pass over him. 17 The sentence is by the decree of the watchers, the decision by the word of the holy ones, **to the end that the living may know that the Most High rules the kingdom of men and gives it to whom he will and sets over it the lowliest of men.**'
      i. A tree described similarly to the tree of life is going to be chopped down.
      ii. The purpose is to ensure that all mankind knows that God is the Most High.

4. Daniel interprets the dream for Nebuchadnezzar.

   a. Daniel 4:20-27 - 20 **The tree you saw**, which grew and became strong, so that its top reached to heaven, and it was visible to the end of the whole earth, 21 whose leaves were beautiful and its fruit abundant, and in which was food for all, under which beasts of the field found shade, and in whose branches the birds of the heavens lived-- 22 **it is you, O king, who have grown and become strong. Your greatness has grown and reaches to heaven, and your dominion to the ends of the earth.** 23 And because the king saw a watcher, a holy one, coming down from heaven and saying, 'Chop down the tree and destroy it, but leave the stump of its roots in the earth, bound with a band of iron and bronze, in the tender grass of the field, and let him be wet with the dew of heaven, and let his portion be with the beasts of the field, till seven periods of time pass over him,' 24 this is the interpretation, O king: It is a decree of the Most High, which has come upon my lord the king, 25 that **you shall be driven from among men, and your dwelling shall be with the beasts of the field. You shall be made to eat grass like an ox, and you shall be wet with the dew of heaven, and seven periods of time shall pass over you, till you know that the Most High rules the kingdom of men and gives it to whom he will. 26 And as it was commanded to leave the stump of the roots of the tree, your kingdom shall be confirmed for you from the time that you know that Heaven rules.** 27 Therefore, O king, let my counsel be acceptable to you: break off your sins by practicing righteousness, and your iniquities by showing mercy to the oppressed, that there may perhaps be a lengthening of your prosperity."

    i. Nebuchadnezzar is the tree that has become strong. It was also arrogant, boastful, self-praising, and self-exalting.
    ii. Nebuchadnezzar would be driven mad, away from normal society until he truly acknowledged that the LORD is God – the Most High.
    iii. Daniel counseled Nebuchadnezzar to repent, humble himself before God, and demonstrate his repentance through doing what is right in God's sight and by not oppressing the poor.

5. Nebuchadnezzar continued in self-praise and arrogance. Daniel's interpretation came to pass.

    a. Daniel 4:28-33 - 28 All this came upon King Nebuchadnezzar. 29 At the end of twelve months he was walking on the roof of the royal palace of Babylon, 30 and the king answered and said, "**Is not this great Babylon, which I have built by my mighty power as a royal residence and for the glory of my majesty?**" 31 While the words were still in the king's mouth, there fell a voice from heaven, "O King Nebuchadnezzar, to you it is spoken: The kingdom has departed from you, 32 and you shall be driven from among men, and your dwelling shall be with the beasts of the field. And you shall be made to eat grass like an ox, and seven periods of time shall pass over you, **until you know that the Most High rules the kingdom of men and gives it to whom he will.**" 33 Immediately the word was fulfilled against Nebuchadnezzar. He was driven from among men and ate grass like an ox, and his body was wet with the dew of heaven till his hair grew as long as eagles' feathers, and his nails were like birds' claws.

        i. Nebuchadnezzar exalted himself and his own strength, power, and influence.
        ii. Note: Nebuchadnezzar vanished from making any royal decrees in the Babylonian historical record for a period of several years.

6. Nebuchadnezzar finally humbled himself and praised God.

    a. Daniel 4:34-37 - 34 **At the end of the days I, Nebuchadnezzar, lifted my eyes to heaven, and my reason returned to me, and I blessed the Most High, and praised and honored him who lives forever, for his dominion is an everlasting dominion, and his kingdom endures from generation to generation; 35 all the inhabitants of the earth are accounted as nothing, and he does according to his will among the host of heaven and among the inhabitants of the earth; and none can stay his hand or say to him, "What have you done?"** 36 At the same time my reason returned to me, and for the glory of my kingdom, my majesty and splendor returned to me. My counselors and my lords sought me, and I was established in my kingdom, and still more greatness was added to me. 37 **Now I, Nebuchadnezzar, praise and extol and honor the King of heaven, for all his works are right and his ways are just; and those who walk in pride he is able to humble.**

        i. Nebuchadnezzar had finally learned to glorify God.

D. Example: Haman

1. Background story of Haman's hubris.

    a. Esther 3:1-6 - 1 After these things King Ahasuerus promoted **Haman the Agagite**, the son of Hammedatha, and **advanced him and set his throne above all the officials who were with him.** 2 And all the king's servants who were at the king's gate bowed down and paid homage to Haman, for the king had so commanded concerning him. **But Mordecai did not bow down or pay homage.** 3 Then the king's servants who were at the king's gate said to Mordecai, "Why do you transgress the king's command?" 4 And when they spoke to him day after day and he would not listen to them, they told Haman, in order to see whether Mordecai's words would stand, for he had told them that he was a Jew. 5 **And when Haman saw that Mordecai did not bow down or pay homage to him, Haman was filled with fury.** 6 **But he disdained to lay hands on Mordecai alone. So, as they had made known to him the people of Mordecai, Haman sought to destroy all the Jews, the people of Mordecai, throughout the whole kingdom of Ahasuerus.**
        i. Haman was the king's top ranking official.
        ii. Haman's hubris was so intense that it was not sufficient just to penalize Mordecai for not paying homage. He scheduled a day for the annihilation of all Jews worldwide.

2. Exalting himself and a banquet with the queen.

    a. Esther 5:11-14 - 11 **And Haman recounted to them the splendor of his riches, the number of his sons, all the promotions with which the king had honored him, and how he had advanced him above the officials and the servants of the king.** 12 Then Haman said, "Even Queen Esther let no one but me come with the king to the feast she prepared. And tomorrow also I am invited by her together with the king. 13 **Yet all this is worth nothing to me, so long as I see Mordecai the Jew sitting at the king's gate.**" 14 Then his wife Zeresh and all his friends said to him, "**Let a gallows fifty cubits high be made**, and in the morning tell the king to have Mordecai hanged upon it. Then go joyfully with the king to the feast." **This idea pleased Haman, and he had the gallows made.**
        i. Haman's pastime was praising himself to his family and friends.
        ii. None of this was sufficient satisfaction for Haman.
        iii. Haman's objective was the destruction of those who refused to exalt him.

3. The man the king delights to honor.

    a. Esther 6:6-13 - 6 **So Haman came in, and the king said to him, "What should be done to the man whom the king delights to honor?" And Haman said to himself, "Whom would the king delight to honor more than me?"** 7 And Haman said to the king, "For the man whom the king delights to honor, 8 let royal robes be brought, which the king has worn, and the horse that the king has ridden, and on whose head a royal crown is set. 9 And let the robes and the horse be handed over to one of the king's most noble officials. Let them dress the man whom the king delights to honor, and let them lead him on the horse through the square of the city, proclaiming before him: 'Thus shall it be done to the man whom the king delights to honor.'" 10 **Then the king said to Haman, "Hurry; take the robes and the horse, as you have said, and do so to Mordecai the Jew,** who sits at the king's gate. Leave out nothing that you have mentioned." 11 So Haman took the robes and the horse, and he dressed Mordecai and led him through the square of the city, proclaiming before him, "Thus shall it be done to the man whom the king delights to honor." 12 Then Mordecai returned to the king's gate. But **Haman hurried to his house, mourning and with his head covered.** 13 And Haman told his

wife Zeresh and all his friends everything that had happened to him. Then his wise men and his wife Zeresh said to him, "**If Mordecai, before whom you have begun to fall, is of the Jewish people, you will not overcome him but will surely fall before him**."
    i. Haman could not conceive of the king wanting to honor anyone other than him. His hubris blinded him to anything other than his own perceived greatness.
    ii. However, the king delighted to honor Haman's enemy. Haman's wife and friends knew this would not turn out well for him.

4. Haman's evil plot exposed and reversed.

    a. Esther 7:3-6 - 3 Then Queen Esther answered, "If I have found favor in your sight, O king, and if it please the king, let my life be granted me for my wish, and my people for my request. 4 **For we have been sold, I and my people, to be destroyed, to be killed, and to be annihilated**. If we had been sold merely as slaves, men and women, I would have been silent, for our affliction is not to be compared with the loss to the king." 5 Then King Ahasuerus said to Queen Esther, "**Who is he, and where is he, who has dared to do this?**" 6 And Esther said, "**A foe and enemy! This wicked Haman!**" Then Haman was terrified before the king and the queen.
        i. Queen Esther exposed Haman as an enemy of her people.

    b. Esther 7:9-10 - 9 Then Harbona, one of the eunuchs in attendance on the king, said, "Moreover, **the gallows that Haman has prepared for Mordecai, whose word saved the king, is standing at Haman's house**, fifty cubits high." And the king said, "**Hang him on that**." 10 **So they hanged Haman on the gallows that he had prepared for Mordecai**. Then the wrath of the king abated.
        i. Haman was hanged on the gallows he had prepared for Mordecai his enemy.

    c. Esther 10:3 - 3 **For Mordecai the Jew was second in rank to King Ahasuerus, and he was great among the Jews and popular with the multitude of his brothers, for he sought the welfare of his people and spoke peace to all his people.**
        i. The king promoted Mordecai to Haman's position, second to him in all the kingdom.

E. The Day of the Lord: The Removal of the Proud & Arrogant

1. The removal of the proud and self-exalting.

    a. Isaiah 2:11-12, 17 - 11 The **haughty looks of man shall be brought low, and the lofty pride of men shall be humbled**, and the LORD alone will be exalted in that day. 12 **For the LORD of hosts has a day against all that is proud and lofty, against all that is lifted up--and it shall be brought low**; ... 17 And **the haughtiness of man shall be humbled, and the lofty pride of men shall be brought low**, and the LORD alone will be exalted in that day.
        i. The proud and haughty will be humbled.

    b. Zephaniah 3:11-13 - 11 "On that day you shall not be put to shame because of the deeds by which you have rebelled against me; for then **I will remove from your midst your proudly exultant ones, and you shall no longer be haughty in my holy mountain**. 12 But **I will leave in your midst a people humble and lowly**. They shall seek refuge in the name of the LORD, 13 those who are left in Israel; **they shall do no injustice and speak no lies, nor shall there be**

found in their mouth a deceitful tongue. For they shall graze and lie down, and none shall make them afraid."
- i. Only the humble will remain.

c. Malachi 4:1-3 - 1 "For behold, the day is coming, burning like an oven, when **all the arrogant and all evildoers will be stubble.** The day that is coming shall set them ablaze, says the LORD of hosts, so that it will leave them neither root nor branch. 2 **But for you who fear my name, the sun of righteousness shall rise with healing in its wings.** You shall go out leaping like calves from the stall. 3 And **you shall tread down the wicked, for they will be ashes under the soles of your feet**, on the day when I act, says the LORD of hosts.
- i. The arrogant and evildoing will be destroyed.
- ii. The humble who fear the Lord will rejoice and trample the wicked.

2. The judgment of Babylon, the symbol of the world's united and total rebellion against God.

a. Revelation 18:2-8 - 2 And he called out with a mighty voice, "**Fallen, fallen is Babylon the great!** She has become a dwelling place for demons, a haunt for every unclean spirit, a haunt for every unclean bird, a haunt for every unclean and detestable beast. 3 **For all nations have drunk the wine of the passion of her sexual immorality, and the kings of the earth have committed immorality with her, and the merchants of the earth have grown rich from the power of her luxurious living.**" 4 Then I heard another voice from heaven saying, "Come out of her, my people, lest you take part in her sins, lest you share in her plagues; 5 for **her sins are heaped high as heaven, and God has remembered her iniquities**. 6 Pay her back as she herself has paid back others, and repay her double for her deeds; mix a double portion for her in the cup she mixed. 7 **As she glorified herself and lived in luxury, so give her a like measure of torment and mourning, since in her heart she says, 'I sit as a queen, I am no widow, and mourning I shall never see.'** 8 For this reason her plagues will come in a single day, death and mourning and famine, and **she will be burned up with fire; for mighty is the Lord God who has judged her.**"
- i. Those who glorify themselves and live for pleasure will be brought down.

3. Mankind's stubborn refusal to repent in spite of seeing miraculous catastrophes.

a. Revelation 9:20-21 - 20 The rest of mankind, who were not killed by these plagues, **did not repent of the works of their hands** nor give up worshiping demons and idols of gold and silver and bronze and stone and wood, which cannot see or hear or walk, 21 **nor did they repent of their murders or their sorceries or their sexual immorality or their thefts**.
- i. Even in the midst of great plagues and disasters, the proud will not repent.

b. Revelation 16:8-11, 21 - 8 The fourth angel poured out his bowl on the sun, and it was allowed to scorch people with fire. 9 They were scorched by the fierce heat, and they **cursed the name of God who had power over these plagues. They did not repent and give him glory**. 10 The fifth angel poured out his bowl on the throne of the beast, and its kingdom was plunged into darkness. People gnawed their tongues in anguish 11 and **cursed the God of heaven for their pain and sores. They did not repent of their deeds**. ... 21 And great hailstones, about one hundred pounds each, fell from heaven on people; and **they cursed God** for the plague of the hail, because the plague was so severe.
- i. In the midst of the wrath of God, the proud will curse God rather than repent.

d. Revelation 21:8 - 8 But **as for the cowardly, the faithless, the detestable, as for murderers, the sexually immoral, sorcerers, idolaters, and all liars**, their portion will be in the lake that burns with fire and sulfur, which is the second death."

F. Messiah and the Rise and Fall of Many

1. Mary's Magnificat.

    a. Luke 1:46-55 - 46 And Mary said, "My soul magnifies the Lord, 47 and my spirit rejoices in God my Savior, 48 for he has looked on the humble estate of his servant. For behold, from now on all generations will call me blessed; 49 for he who is mighty has done great things for me, and holy is his name. 50 And **his mercy is for those who fear him from generation to generation**. 51 He has shown strength with his arm; **he has scattered the proud in the thoughts of their hearts; 52 he has brought down the mighty from their thrones and exalted those of humble estate**; 53 **he has filled the hungry with good things, and the rich he has sent away empty. 54 He has helped his servant Israel, in remembrance of his mercy**, 55 as he spoke to our fathers, to Abraham and to his offspring forever."
        i. God is merciful to those who fear Him. God exalts the humble. God feeds the hungry.
        ii. God brings down the proud and oppressive. God empties the rich and arrogant.

2. The person of Jesus causes people to rise or to fall.

    a. Luke 2:34-35 - 34 And Simeon blessed them and said to Mary his mother, "**Behold, this child is appointed for the fall and rising of many in Israel**, and for a sign that is opposed 35 (and a sword will pierce through your own soul also), **so that thoughts from many hearts may be revealed**."

    b. Jesus is the cornerstone AND the rock of offense.
        i. Isaiah 28:16 - 16 therefore thus says the Lord GOD, "Behold, I am the one who has laid as a foundation in Zion, **a stone, a tested stone, a precious cornerstone, of a sure foundation**: 'Whoever believes will not be in haste.'
        ii. Isaiah 8:14-15 - 14 And he will become a sanctuary and a **stone of offense and a rock of stumbling** to both houses of Israel, **a trap and a snare** to the inhabitants of Jerusalem. 15 And **many shall stumble on it. They shall fall and be broken**; they shall be snared and taken."

3. John the Baptist's ministry prepared the way for the Lord.

    a. Matthew 3:2-3 - 2 "**Repent, for the kingdom of heaven is at hand**." 3 For this is he who was spoken of by the prophet Isaiah when he said, "The voice of one crying in the wilderness: 'Prepare the way of the Lord; make his paths straight.'" (See also Luke 3:3-6; Mark 1:2-6.)
        i. Isaiah 40:3-5 - 3 A voice cries: "In the wilderness prepare the way of the LORD; make straight in the desert a highway for our God. 4 **Every valley shall be lifted up, and every mountain and hill be made low; the uneven ground shall become level, and the rough places a plain**. 5 And the glory of the LORD shall be revealed, and all flesh shall see it together, for the mouth of the LORD has spoken."
        ii. The Messiah will level everything high and exalted, strengthen the oppressed, straighten everything crooked, and smooth out everything rough.
        iii. To prepare for the Lord's coming, the proud should repent humble themselves.

G. God Saves the Humble

1. Psalm 76:8-9 - 8 From the heavens you uttered judgment; the earth feared and was still, 9 when **God arose to establish judgment, to save all the humble of the earth**. Selah

2. Psalm 149:4 - 4 For the LORD takes pleasure in his people; **he adorns the humble with salvation**.

3. Psalm 25:8-9 - 8 Good and upright is the LORD; therefore **he instructs sinners in the way**. 9 **He leads the humble** in what is right, and **teaches the humble his way**.

4. Zephaniah 2:3 - 3 Seek the LORD, **all you humble of the land**, who do his just commands; seek righteousness; **seek humility; perhaps you may be hidden on the day of the anger of the LORD**.

5. James 4:6, 10 - 6 But he gives more grace. Therefore it says, "**God opposes the proud but gives grace to the humble**." ... 10 Humble yourselves before the Lord, and he will exalt you.

6. 1 Peter 5:6 - 6 **Humble yourselves**, therefore, under the mighty hand of God so that at the proper time he may exalt you,

7. Isaiah 66:1-2, 5-6 - 1 Thus says the LORD: "Heaven is my throne, and the earth is my footstool; what is the house that you would build for me, and what is the place of my rest? 2 All these things my hand has made, and so all these things came to be, declares the LORD. **But this is the one to whom I will look: he who is humble and contrite in spirit and trembles at my word**. ... 5 **Hear the word of the LORD, you who tremble at his word**: "Your brothers who hate you and cast you out for my name's sake have said, 'Let the LORD be glorified, that we may see your joy'; but it is they who shall be put to shame. 6 'The sound of an uproar from the city! A sound from the temple! **The sound of the LORD, rendering recompense to his enemies!**

H. Worship & Rejoicing at God's Judgment of the Proud

1. God's people worshipping with song and music while God brings judgment on the nations.

    a. Isaiah 30:27-33 - 27 Behold, the name of the LORD comes from afar, burning with his anger, and in thick rising smoke; **his lips are full of fury, and his tongue is like a devouring fire**; 28 **his breath is like an overflowing stream** that reaches up to the neck; to **sift the nations with the sieve of destruction**, and to place on the jaws of the peoples a bridle that leads astray. 29 **You shall have a song as in the night when a holy feast is kept, and gladness of heart, as when one sets out to the sound of the flute** to go to the mountain of the LORD, to the Rock of Israel. 30 And the LORD will cause his majestic voice to be heard and the descending blow of his arm to be seen, **in furious anger and a flame of devouring fire, with a cloudburst and storm and hailstones**. 31 The Assyrians will be terror-stricken at the voice of the LORD, when he strikes with his rod. 32 And **every stroke of the appointed staff that the LORD lays on them will be to the sound of tambourines and lyres**. Battling with brandished arm, he will fight with them. 33 For a burning place has long been prepared; indeed, for the king it is made ready, its pyre made deep and wide, with fire and wood in abundance; the breath of the LORD, like a stream of sulfur, kindles it.
        i. God's people worship Him with flutes, tambourines, and lyres while He shakes the nations with destruction.
        ii. A victory song like the Israelites sang over Pharaoh. (See Exodus 15)

                01. Exodus 15:20-21 - 20 Then Miriam the prophetess, the sister of Aaron, **took a tambourine** in her hand, and all the women went out after her **with tambourines and dancing**. 21 And Miriam sang to them: "**Sing to the LORD, for he has triumphed gloriously; the horse and his rider he has thrown into the sea**."
            iii. A victory song like the people sang after David conquered Goliath and other enemies.
                01. 1 Samuel 18:7 - 7 And the women **sang to one another as they celebrated**, "Saul has struck down his thousands, and David his ten thousands."

2. Rejoicing in the judgments of God. This is God's vengeance for the shed blood of the innocent and martyrs, and against all wrongdoing and evil.

    a. Revelation 11:16-18 - 16 And the twenty-four elders who sit on their thrones before God fell on their faces and worshiped God, 17 saying, "**We give thanks to you, Lord God Almighty**, who is and who was, for you have taken your great power and begun to reign. 18 **The nations raged, but your wrath came, and the time for the dead to be judged, and for rewarding your servants, the prophets and saints, and those who fear your name, both small and great, and for destroying the destroyers of the earth**."
        i. We will rejoice with God on the day of judgment. We will not have sorrow over those who refused to humble themselves after being given many opportunities to do so.
            01. This is why it is so important for us to give people those opportunities while there is still time.

    b. Revelation 16:5-7 - 5 And I heard the angel in charge of the waters say, "**Just are you, O Holy One**, who is and who was, for you brought these judgments. 6 **For they have shed the blood of saints and prophets**, and you have given them blood to drink. **It is what they deserve!**" 7 And I heard the altar saying, "Yes, Lord God the Almighty, **true and just are your judgments!**"
        i. We will rejoice in the justice of God for His vengeance against the wicked.
            01. This is why it is so important that we tell the wicked to repent while there is still time.

    c. Revelation 19:1-5 - 1 After this I heard what seemed to be the loud voice of a great multitude in heaven, crying out, "Hallelujah! Salvation and glory and power belong to our God, 2 for **his judgments are true and just; for he has judged the great prostitute who corrupted the earth with her immorality, and has avenged on her the blood of his servants**." 3 Once more they cried out, "Hallelujah! **The smoke from her goes up forever and ever**."
        i. We will rejoice in God's righteous and true judgment of the people of this world.
            01. This is why we must tell the world of His redemption while there is still time.

3. Rejoice and execute judgments with God.

    a. Psalm 52:1-7 - 1 Why do you boast of evil, O mighty man? The steadfast love of God endures all the day. 2 Your tongue plots destruction, like a sharp razor, you worker of deceit. 3 You love evil more than good, and lying more than speaking what is right. Selah 4 You love all words that devour, O deceitful tongue. 5 **But God will break you down forever**; he will snatch and tear you from your tent; he will uproot you from the land of the living. Selah 6 **The righteous shall see and fear, and shall laugh at him, saying,** 7 "**See the man who would not make God his refuge, but trusted in the abundance of his riches and sought refuge in his own destruction!**"

b. Psalm 58:10-11 - 10 **The righteous will rejoice when he sees the vengeance; he will bathe his feet in the blood of the wicked.** 11 Mankind will say, "Surely there is a reward for the righteous; surely there is a God who judges on earth."

c. Psalm 137:8-9 - 8 O daughter of Babylon, doomed to be destroyed, **blessed shall he be who repays you with what you have done to us!** 9 Blessed shall he be who takes your little ones and dashes them against the rock!

d. Psalm 149:4-9 - 4 For the LORD takes pleasure in his people; he adorns the humble with salvation. 5 Let the godly exult in glory; let them sing for joy on their beds. 6 Let the high praises of God be in their throats and two-edged swords in their hands, 7 **to execute vengeance on the nations and punishments on the peoples,** 8 **to bind their kings with chains and their nobles with fetters of iron,** 9 **to execute on them the judgment written! This is honor for all his godly ones.** Praise the LORD!

e. Revelation 19:11-16 - 11 Then I saw heaven opened, and behold, a white horse! The one sitting on it is called Faithful and True, **and in righteousness he judges and makes war.** 12 His eyes are like a flame of fire, and on his head are many diadems, and he has a name written that no one knows but himself. 13 He is clothed in a robe dipped in blood, and the name by which he is called is The Word of God. 14 **And the armies of heaven, arrayed in fine linen, white and pure, were following him on white horses.** 15 **From his mouth comes a sharp sword with which to strike down the nations, and he will rule them with a rod of iron. He will tread the winepress of the fury of the wrath of God the Almighty.** 16 On his robe and on his thigh he has a name written, King of kings and Lord of lords.
   i. We will execute judgment with the Lord.

4. Resurrection of the just and the reward of the saints.

   a. Daniel 12:1-3 - 1 "At that time shall arise Michael, the great prince who has charge of your people. And there shall be a time of trouble, such as never has been since there was a nation till that time. **But at that time your people shall be delivered, everyone whose name shall be found written in the book. 2 And many of those who sleep in the dust of the earth shall awake, some to everlasting life, and some to shame and everlasting contempt.** 3 And those who are wise shall shine like the brightness of the sky above; and those who turn many to righteousness, like the stars forever and ever.
      i. Only those who have humbled themselves before God to do things His way will be resurrected to eternal life.
      ii. All arrogant, proud, rebels against God will be resurrected to eternal contempt.

   b. Romans 2:5-11 - 5 But because of your hard and impenitent heart you are storing up wrath for yourself on the day of wrath when God's righteous judgment will be revealed. 6 **He will render to each one according to his works: 7 to those who by patience in well-doing seek for glory and honor and immortality, he will give eternal life; 8 but for those who are self-seeking and do not obey the truth, but obey unrighteousness, there will be wrath and fury.** 9 There will be tribulation and distress for every human being who does evil, the Jew first and also the Greek, 10 but glory and honor and peace for everyone who does good, the Jew first and also the Greek. 11 For God shows no partiality.
      i. We still have the opportunity to shift our focus to persevering in God's ways and doing what is right in His sight by obeying righteousness, and speaking the truth.
      ii. If we remain selfish, proud, self-seeking, we will be subject to God's wrath and fury.

c. Revelation 20:11-15 - 11 Then I saw a great white throne and him who was seated on it. From his presence earth and sky fled away, and no place was found for them. 12 **And I saw the dead, great and small, standing before the throne, and books were opened. Then another book was opened, which is the book of life. And the dead were judged by what was written in the books, according to what they had done.** 13 And the sea gave up the dead who were in it, Death and Hades gave up the dead who were in them, **and they were judged, each one of them, according to what they had done.** 14 Then Death and Hades were thrown into the lake of fire. This is the second death, the lake of fire. 15 **And if anyone's name was not found written in the book of life, he was thrown into the lake of fire.**
    i. We will give account for the life we have lived and whether our deeds display arrogant rebellion against God or humble submission to Him.

d. Revelation 21:1-3 - 1 Then I saw **a new heaven and a new earth**, for the first heaven and the first earth had passed away, and the sea was no more. 2 And I saw the holy city, new Jerusalem, coming down out of heaven from God, **prepared as a bride adorned for her husband.** 3 And I heard a loud voice from the throne saying, "**Behold, the dwelling place of God is with man. He will dwell with them, and they will be his people, and God himself will be with them as their God.**"
    i. Those who have purified their lives from the pride, evil, and ways of this world will rejoice as a Bride with her Bridegroom, Jesus.

Unit Four: Humble Yourself Before God, Part One: Turning

> Be not wise in your own eyes; fear the LORD, and turn away from evil.
>
> Proverbs 3:7

Pre-Note: God created the world, is all-powerful, all-knowing, and sovereign over all creation. He lowered Himself to put on flesh and die on a cross to make it possible for us to draw near to Him. This is because of HIS goodness, not our own merit or anything we have done to deserve it. Moreover, if He had not done it, we would be condemned to His wrath and eternal fire with the wicked.

> *Ephesians 2:11-13 - Therefore remember that at one time you Gentiles in the flesh, called "the uncircumcision" by what is called the circumcision, which is made in the flesh by hands-- remember that you were at that time separated from Christ, alienated from the commonwealth of Israel and strangers to the covenants of promise, having no hope and without God in the world. But now in Christ Jesus you who once were far off have been brought near by the blood of Christ.*

> *Romans 5:1-2, 6-8 - 1 Therefore, since we have been justified by faith, we have peace with God through our Lord Jesus Christ. Through him we have also obtained access by faith into this grace in which we stand, and we rejoice in hope of the glory of God. ... For while we were still weak, at the right time Christ died for the ungodly. For one will scarcely die for a righteous person--though perhaps for a good person one would dare even to die-- but God shows his love for us in that while we were still sinners, Christ died for us.*

> *Colossians 1:21-23 - And you, who once were alienated and hostile in mind, doing evil deeds, he has now reconciled in his body of flesh by his death, in order to present you holy and blameless and above reproach before him, if indeed you continue in the faith, stable and steadfast, not shifting from the hope of the gospel that you heard, which has been proclaimed in all creation under heaven, and of which I, Paul, became a minister.*

We are not on equal footing with God. Our faith in Jesus' death and resurrection gives us peace with God and access to Him that we would otherwise have NO RIGHT to have.

A. Thanksgiving, Praise, & Worship

1. Thanksgiving is saying thank you to God for all He does for us.

    a. It acknowledges with gratitude that what we have, what we are able to do, and the circumstances of our life are attributed to something other than ourselves, namely to God.

    b. It acknowledges with gratitude that God sees us, cares for us, and is sovereign over all things pertaining to us.

c. It gives God the glory He deserves.

2. Give God the praise and worship He deserves as Creator, King, and gracious Redeemer.

   a. Psalm 150:6 - 6 **Let everything that has breath praise the LORD!** Praise the LORD!

   b. Nehemiah 9:6 - 6 "**You are the LORD, you alone.** You have made heaven, the heaven of heavens, with all their host, the earth and all that is on it, the seas and all that is in them; and you preserve all of them; and the host of heaven worships you.

   c. Psalm 29:1-2 - 1 Ascribe to the LORD, O heavenly beings, ascribe to the LORD glory and strength. 2 **Ascribe to the LORD the glory due his name; worship the LORD in the splendor of holiness.**

   d. Psalm 22:28 - 28 For **kingship belongs to the LORD**, and he rules over the nations.

   e. Revelation 5:12-13 - 12 saying with a loud voice, "**Worthy is the Lamb who was slain, to receive power and wealth and wisdom and might and honor and glory and blessing!**" 13 And I heard every creature in heaven and on earth and under the earth and in the sea, and all that is in them, saying, "**To him who sits on the throne and to the Lamb be blessing and honor and glory and might forever and ever!**"

3. Be the one who gives God thanks for what He has done for you. Praise is better than a sacrifice.

   a. Luke 17:12-18 - 12 And as he entered a village, he was met by ten lepers, who stood at a distance 13 and lifted up their voices, saying, "Jesus, Master, have mercy on us." 14 When he saw them he said to them, "Go and show yourselves to the priests." And as they went they were cleansed. 15 **Then one of them, when he saw that he was healed, turned back, praising God with a loud voice; 16 and he fell on his face at Jesus' feet, giving him thanks.** Now he was a Samaritan. 17 Then Jesus answered, "Were not ten cleansed? Where are the nine? 18 **Was no one found to return and give praise to God except this foreigner?**"
      i. Ten lepers received healing. Only one came back to give thanks.

   b. Psalm 50:12-15, 23 - 12 "If I were hungry, I would not tell you, for the world and its fullness are mine. 13 Do I eat the flesh of bulls or drink the blood of goats? 14 **Offer to God a sacrifice of thanksgiving**, and perform your vows to the Most High, 15 and call upon me in the day of trouble; I will deliver you, and you shall glorify me." ... 23 **The one who offers thanksgiving as his sacrifice glorifies me**; to one who orders his way rightly I will show the salvation of God!"

4. Let the redeemed of the Lord say so. Testify to others of the goodness of God towards you and how He saved you from the path of destruction and death.

   a. Psalm 107:1-2 - 1 Oh **give thanks to the LORD, for he is good**, for his steadfast love endures forever! 2 **Let the redeemed of the LORD say so**, whom he has redeemed from trouble.

   b. Psalm 34:1-2 - 1 Of David, when he changed his behavior before Abimelech, so that he drove him out, and he went away. **I will bless the LORD at all times; his praise shall continually be in my mouth. 2 My soul makes its boast in the LORD**; let the humble hear and be glad.

   c. Psalm 103:1-5 - 1 **Bless the LORD, O my soul, and all that is within me, bless his holy name!** 2 Bless the LORD, O my soul, and forget not all his benefits, 3 who forgives all your iniquity, who heals all your diseases, 4 who redeems your life from the pit, who crowns you with steadfast love and mercy, 5 who satisfies you with good so that your youth is renewed like the eagle's.

5. Silence your flesh in His presence.

   a. Psalm 46:10 - 10 "**Be still, and know that I am God.** I will be exalted among the nations, I will be exalted in the earth!"

   b. Habakkuk 2:20 - 20 But the LORD is in his holy temple; **let all the earth keep silence before him."**

   c. Job 40:3-5 - 3 Then Job answered the LORD and said: 4 "**Behold, I am of small account; what shall I answer you? I lay my hand on my mouth**. 5 I have spoken once, and I will not answer; twice, but I will proceed no further."

B. Confession of Sin

1. Confession of sin agrees with God about our true position before Him.

   a. Psalm 8:3-4 - 3 When I look at your heavens, the work of your fingers, the moon and the stars, which you have set in place, 4 **what is man that you are mindful of him**, and the son of man that you care for him?

   b. Luke 18:13-14 - 13 But the tax collector, standing far off, would not even lift up his eyes to heaven, but beat his breast, saying, **'God, be merciful to me, a sinner!'**

2. Confession of sin identifies sin as sin. Confession is admitting that we have done wrong, violated God's ways, been selfish, and fallen short of God's standard of perfection. Confession is seeking the Lord for mercy and forgiveness that only He can give us.

   a. Psalm 51:1-4 - 1 *A Psalm of David, when Nathan the prophet went to him, after he had gone in to Bathsheba.* **Have mercy on me, O God**, according to your steadfast love; according to your abundant mercy **blot out my transgressions**. 2 Wash me thoroughly from my iniquity, and **cleanse me from my sin!** 3 For **I know my transgressions**, and **my sin is ever before me**. 4 **Against you, you only, have I sinned and done what is evil in your sight**, so that you may be justified in your words and blameless in your judgment.

   b. Psalm 32:2-5 - 2 Blessed is the man against whom the LORD counts no iniquity, and in whose spirit there is no deceit. 3 For when I kept silent, my bones wasted away through my groaning all day long. 4 For day and night your hand was heavy upon me; my strength was dried up as by the heat of summer. Selah 5 **I acknowledged my sin to you, and I did not cover my iniquity; I said, "I will confess my transgressions to the LORD**," and you forgave the iniquity of my sin. Selah

   c. Psalm 38:1-8, 18 - 1 O LORD, rebuke me not in your anger, nor discipline me in your wrath! 2 For your arrows have sunk into me, and your hand has come down on me. 3 There is no soundness in my flesh **because of your indignation**; there is no health in my bones **because of my sin**. 4 **For my iniquities have gone over my head; like a heavy burden, they are too heavy for me**. 5 My wounds stink and fester **because of my foolishness**, 6 I am utterly bowed down and prostrate; all the day I go about mourning. 7 For my sides are filled with burning, and there is no soundness in my flesh. 8 I am feeble and crushed; I groan because of the tumult of my heart. ... 18 **I confess my iniquity; I am sorry for my sin**.

    d. Luke 15:21 - 21 And the son said to him, **'Father, I have sinned against heaven and before you**. I am no longer worthy to be called your son.'

    e. Mark 1:5 - 5 And all the country of Judea and all Jerusalem were going out to him [John the Baptist] and **were being baptized by him in the river Jordan, confessing their sins**.

3. Confession of sin, by calling sin out for what it is, helps us towards renouncing sin. It is the path to receiving forgiveness and walking in freedom.

    a. 1 John 1:8-10 - 8 If we say we have no sin, we deceive ourselves, and the truth is not in us. 9 **If we confess our sins, he is faithful and just to forgive us our sins and to cleanse us from all unrighteousness**. 10 If we say we have not sinned, we make him a liar, and his word is not in us.

    b. Proverbs 28:13 - 13 Whoever conceals his transgressions will not prosper, but **he who confesses and forsakes them will obtain mercy**.

    c. James 5:16 - 16 Therefore, **confess your sins to one another and pray for one another**, that you may be healed. The prayer of a righteous person has great power as it is working.

C. The Fear of the Lord

1. The fear of the Lord is simply taking God seriously.

> Fear: Hebrew-H3374: *yir'a*: 1. Fear, terror, fearing. 2. Awesome or terrifying thing causing fear. 3. Respect, reverence, piety. 4. Revered.

    a. Fear of the Lord is a proper, healthy reverence for God as the all-powerful Creator and sovereign King over everything.

    b. Fear of the Lord is a knowing that God is watching my every move, knows the motives of my heart, and is ultimately the Judge I will stand before to give account for my life.

2. An encounter with the true Jesus should leave us awed with Him, humbled by His holiness, and disgusted with our own filth and unworthiness.

    a. Luke 5:8 - 8 But when Simon Peter saw it, he fell down at Jesus' knees, saying, "**Depart from me, for I am a sinful man, O Lord**."

    b. Isaiah 6:3, 5 - 3 And one called to another and said: "Holy, holy, holy is the LORD of hosts; the whole earth is full of his glory!" ... 5 And I said: "**Woe is me! For I am lost; for I am a man of unclean lips, and I dwell in the midst of a people of unclean lips**; for my eyes have seen the King, the LORD of hosts!"

    c. Acts 2:36-38 - 36 Let all the house of Israel therefore know for certain that God has made him both Lord and Christ, this Jesus whom you crucified." 37 Now when they heard this **they were cut to the heart**, and said to Peter and the rest of the apostles, "Brothers, **what shall we do?**"

38 And Peter said to them, "**Repent and be baptized every one of you in the name of Jesus Christ for the forgiveness of your sins, and you will receive the gift of the Holy Spirit.**

3. By the fear of the Lord, we turn from evil.

    i. Psalm 34:11-14 - 11 Come, O children, listen to me; **I will teach you the fear of the LORD.** 12 What man is there who desires life and loves many days, that he may see good? 13 **Keep your tongue from evil and your lips from speaking deceit.** 14 **Turn away from evil and do good; seek peace and pursue it.**

    ii. Proverbs 8:13 - 13 **The fear of the LORD is hatred of evil.** Pride and arrogance and the way of evil and perverted speech I hate.

    iii. Job 28:28 - 28 And he said to man, 'Behold, the **fear of the Lord, that is wisdom**, and **to turn away from evil is understanding.**'

    iv. Proverbs 3:7 - 7 Be not wise in your own eyes; **fear the LORD, and turn away from evil.**

   b. Scriptures about the Fear of the Lord.
      www.manifestinternational.com/free

      Or click the image to download.

D. Repentance

1. Repentance means to stop doing things your way and start doing things God's way. It means to turn around, change direction, do it differently.

    > Repent: Hebrew-H7725: *sub*: 1. To return or turn back. 2. To turn back to God. 3. To turn oneself. 4. To cease from or leave off.

    > Repent: Greek-G3340: *matanoeo*: 1. To change one's mind. 2. To change one's mind for the better, with hearty abhorrence and amends for one's past sins. 3. To think differently or reconsider.

2. Jesus' primary message and the message of the apostles was "Repent for the Kingdom of Heaven is at hand!"

    a. Matthew 4:17 - 17 From that time Jesus began to preach, saying, "**Repent, for the kingdom of heaven is at hand.**"

    b. Mark 1:14-15 - 14 Now after John was arrested, Jesus came into Galilee, proclaiming the gospel of God, 15 and saying, "The time is fulfilled, and **the kingdom of God is at hand; repent and believe in the gospel.**"

- c. Luke 24:45-47 - 45 Then he opened their minds to understand the Scriptures, 46 and said to them, "Thus it is written, that the Christ should suffer and on the third day rise from the dead, 47 and that **repentance for the forgiveness of sins should be proclaimed in his name to all nations**, beginning from Jerusalem.

- d. Acts 2:38, 40 - 38 And Peter said to them, "**Repent and be baptized** every one of you in the name of Jesus Christ for the forgiveness of your sins, and you will receive the gift of the Holy Spirit. ... 40 And with many other words he bore witness and continued to exhort them, saying, "**Save yourselves from this crooked generation**."

- e. Acts 17:30-31 - 30 The times of ignorance God overlooked, **but now he commands all people everywhere to repent**, 31 because he has fixed a day on which he will judge the world in righteousness by a man whom he has appointed; and of this he has given assurance to all by raising him from the dead."

3. Jesus came to offer a way of salvation, through repentance, to the whole world that is already condemned and doomed to the wrath of God and the day of judgment. He did not come to condemn what is already condemned, He came to save.

   - a. John 3:16-18, 36 - 16 "For God so loved the world, that he gave his only Son, that whoever believes in him should not perish but have eternal life. 17 For God did not send his Son into the world to condemn the world, but in order that the world might be saved through him. 18 Whoever believes in him is not condemned, but **whoever does not believe is condemned already, because he has not believed in the name of the only Son of God**. ... 36 Whoever believes in the Son has eternal life; **whoever does not obey the Son shall not see life, but the wrath of God remains on him.**

   - b. Jesus warned that continued repentance was necessary for people to escape the final judgment, even after He had initially shown them great mercy.
     - i. John 8:10-11 - 10 Jesus stood up and said to her, "Woman, where are they? Has no one condemned you?" 11 She said, "No one, Lord." And Jesus said, "Neither do I condemn you; **go, and from now on sin no more**."
     - ii. John 5:13-14 - 13 Now the man who had been healed did not know who it was, for Jesus had withdrawn, as there was a crowd in the place. 14 Afterward Jesus found him in the temple and said to him, "See, you are well! **Sin no more, that nothing worse may happen to you.**"

   - c. We must continue in repentance to maintain our position in Christ.
     - i. 2 Timothy 2:11-13- 11 The saying is trustworthy, for: If we have died with him, we will also live with him; 12 if we endure, we will also reign with him; **if we deny him, he also will deny us**; 13 if we are faithless, he remains faithful-- for he cannot deny himself.
     - ii. Romans 11:20-22 - 20 That is true. They were broken off because of their unbelief, but you stand fast through faith. So **do not become proud, but fear**. 21 For if God did not spare the natural branches, **neither will he spare you.** 22 Note then the kindness and the severity of God: severity toward those who have fallen, but God's kindness to you, **provided you continue in his kindness. Otherwise you too will be cut off.**
     - iii. Colossians 1:23 - 23 ...**if indeed you continue in the faith**, stable and steadfast, **not shifting from the hope of the gospel that you heard**, which has been proclaimed in all creation under heaven, and of which I, Paul, became a minister.
     - iv. 1 Corinthians 10:5-12 - 5 Nevertheless, **with most of them [Israelites in the wilderness] God was not pleased, for they were overthrown in the wilderness.** 6 Now these things took

place as **examples for us, that we might not desire evil as they did.** 7 Do not be idolaters as some of them were; as it is written, "The people sat down to eat and drink and rose up to play." 8 We must not indulge in sexual immorality as some of them did, and twenty-three thousand fell in a single day. 9 We must not put Christ to the test, as some of them did and were destroyed by serpents, 10 nor grumble, as some of them did and were destroyed by the Destroyer. 11 **Now these things happened to them as an example, but they were written down for our instruction**, on whom the end of the ages has come. 12 Therefore **let anyone who thinks that he stands take heed lest he fall.**

    d. Example: The Jonah and the People of Nineveh:
        i. God sent Jonah to Nineveh to proclaim that it was doomed to destruction if the people did not repent. Jonah proclaimed disaster to Nineveh.
        ii. When the King of Nineveh heard this, he Nineveh removed his royal attire, covered himself with sackcloth, and proclaimed a city-wide fast for all people and animals as an act of contrition and humbling themselves before God in hope that God would relent from destruction. They believed God and repented of their sin.
        iii. When God saw that they turned from their evil ways, He relented of the disaster that he had determined for them. (Jonah 3.)
        iv. However, in due time, the people of Nineveh returned to their sins and God could no longer extend His mercy to them. The city was totally destroyed forever. (See Book of Nahum.)

4. We must be born again by the regeneration of the Holy Spirit. Those who claim to believe the Lord must turn from sin and purify their lives in holiness.

    a. John 3:3, 5-6 - 3 Jesus answered him, "Truly, truly, I say to you, **unless one is born again he cannot see the kingdom of God.**" ... 5 Jesus answered, "Truly, truly, I say to you, **unless one is born of water and the Spirit, he cannot enter the kingdom of God.** 6 That which is born of the flesh is flesh, and that which is born of the Spirit is spirit.

    b. 2 Timothy 2:19 - 19 But God's firm foundation stands, bearing this seal: "The Lord knows those who are his," and, "**Let everyone who names the name of the Lord depart from iniquity.**"

    c. 1 John 3:2-9 - 2 Beloved, we are God's children now, and what we will be has not yet appeared; but we know that when he appears we shall be like him, because we shall see him as he is. 3 And **everyone who thus hopes in him purifies himself as he is pure.** 4 **Everyone who makes a practice of sinning also practices lawlessness**; sin is lawlessness. 5 You know that he appeared in order to take away sins, and in him there is no sin. 6 **No one who abides in him keeps on sinning**; no one who keeps on sinning has either seen him or known him. 7 Little children, let no one deceive you. Whoever practices righteousness is righteous, as he is righteous. 8 **Whoever makes a practice of sinning is of the devil, for the devil has been sinning from the beginning.** The reason the Son of God appeared was to destroy the works of the devil. 9 **No one born of God makes a practice of sinning**, for God's seed abides in him; and he cannot keep on sinning, **because he has been born of God.**

5. We must make every effort to purify our lives in repentance and offer our lives totally to God for His purposes rather than our own. We do this out of thankfulness for God's mercy, not out of religious obligation, technique, or performance.

    a. 2 Peter 1:5-9 - 5 For this very reason, **make every effort to supplement your faith** with virtue, and virtue with knowledge, 6 and knowledge with self-control, and self-control with steadfastness, and steadfastness with godliness, 7 and godliness with brotherly affection, and brotherly affection with love. 8 For if these qualities are yours and are increasing, **they keep you from being ineffective or unfruitful in the knowledge of our Lord Jesus Christ**. 9 For **whoever lacks these qualities is so nearsighted that he is blind**, having forgotten that he was cleansed from his former sins.

    b. 1 Peter 1:14-16 - 14 As obedient children, **do not be conformed to the passions of your former ignorance**, 15 **but as he who called you is holy, you also be holy in all your conduct**, 16 since it is written, "You shall be holy, for I am holy."

    c. Philippians 2:12-13 - 12 Therefore, my beloved, as you have always obeyed, so now, not only as in my presence but much more in my absence, **work out your own salvation with fear and trembling**, 13 for **it is God who works in you, both to will and to work for his good pleasure**.

    d. 2 Timothy 2:22 - 22 So **flee youthful passions and pursue righteousness, faith, love, and peace**, along with those who call on the Lord from a pure heart.

    e. Example: King Josiah. (2 Kings 22; 2 Chronicles 34.)
        i. In the days of Josiah, the Book of Law was discovered in the Temple as it was being repaired. When the Law was ready to Josiah, he tore his clothes in repentance and fear of the Lord, knowing that God's people were in horrid rebellion against God's Law and should rightfully be under His judgment.
        ii. Josiah took immediate steps to correct Israel's disobedience and lack of adherence to God's commands.
        iii. Josiah sent for a word from the prophetess Huldah. She confirmed that judgment from the Lord would come.
        iv. But because Josiah's heart was tender and he humbled himself, the disaster would not come in his day.

6. Genuine repentance is demonstrated by what we do – by our actions. We must bear fruit in keeping with repentance.

    a. Luke 3:8a-18 - 8 **Bear fruits in keeping with repentance**. ... 9 Even now the axe is laid to the root of the trees. Every tree therefore that does not bear good fruit is cut down and thrown into the fire." 10 And the crowds asked him, "What then shall we do?" 11 And he answered them, "**Whoever has two tunics is to share with him who has none, and whoever has food is to do likewise**." 12 Tax collectors also came to be baptized and said to him, "Teacher, what shall we do?" 13 And he said to them, "**Collect no more than you are authorized to do**." 14 Soldiers also asked him, "And we, what shall we do?" And he said to them, "**Do not extort money from anyone by threats or by false accusation, and be content with your wages**." 15 As the people were in expectation, and all were questioning in their hearts concerning John, whether he might be the Christ, 16 John answered them all, saying, "I baptize you with water, but he who is mightier than I is coming, the strap of whose sandals I am not worthy to untie. He will baptize you with the Holy Spirit and fire. 17 **His winnowing fork is in his hand, to clear his threshing floor and to gather the wheat into his barn, but the chaff he will burn with unquenchable fire**." 18 So with many other exhortations he preached good news to the people.

    b. James 2:14-18 - 14 What good is it, my brothers, **if someone says he has faith but does not have works? Can that faith save him?** 15 If a brother or sister is poorly clothed and lacking in daily food, 16 and one of you says to them, "Go in peace, be warmed and filled," without giving them the things needed for the body, what good is that? 17 So also **faith by itself, if it does not have works, is dead**. 18 But someone will say, "You have faith and I have works." Show me your faith apart from your works, and **I will show you my faith by my works**.

    c. Example: Zacchaeus the tax collector: (Luke 19:1-10.)
        i. Out of joy and thankfulness for Jesus' calling and salvation, Zacchaeus willingly offered to give half of his goods to the poor and to restore four-fold anything he had taken by fraudulent means.

    d. Example: Manasseh, the evil king of Judah. (2 Chronicles 33.)
        i. Manasseh was an evil king who committed greater abominations than any other king, including offering children in the fires of foreign gods and setting up altars to other gods in the Temple of God.
        ii. God tried to warn Manasseh, but he would not listen. Therefore, God had him exiled and put in foreign prison.
        iii. From there, Manasseh greatly humbled himself and prayed to the Lord.
        iv. Therefore, the Lord restored him to his land, to Jerusalem, and to his position as King of Judah.
        v. After that, Manasseh tore down the foreign idols, rebuilt the city, restored the altar of the Temple, and commanded the people to serve the Lord.

E. Obedience & Submission to God

    1. Obedience means doing what someone else commands. Submission means ordering yourself to do things someone else's way.

> Obedience: Greek-G5218: *hypakoe*: 1. Obedience. Compliance. Submission. 2. Obedience rendered to anyone's counsels and requirements.
>
> Obedience: compliance with an order, request, or law or submission to another's authority. (Dictionary.com)
>
> Submit: Greek-G5293: *hypotasso*: 1. Arrange under, to subordinate. 2. To subject one's self, obey. 3. To submit to one's control. 4. To yield to one's admonition or advice. *This word was a Greek military term meaning "to arrange [troop divisions] in a military fashion under the command of a leader". In non-military use, it was "a voluntary attitude of giving in, cooperating, assuming responsibility, and carrying a burden".*

    a. Proverbs 3:5-6 NIV - 5 Trust in the LORD with all your heart and lean not on your own understanding; 6 **in all your ways submit to him**, and he will make your paths straight.

    b. Ecclesiastes 12:13-14 - 13 The end of the matter; all has been heard. **Fear God and keep his commandments, for this is the whole duty of man**. 14 For God will bring every deed into judgment, with every secret thing, whether good or evil.

    c. Example: King Saul learned that obedience is better than sacrifice. Self-will is idolatry and rebellion against God.
        i. 1 Samuel 15:22-23 - 22 And Samuel said, "Has the LORD as great delight in burnt offerings and sacrifices, as in **obeying the voice of the LORD?** Behold, **to obey is better than sacrifice, and to listen than the fat of rams**. 23 For rebellion is as the sin of

divination, and presumption is as iniquity and idolatry. Because you have rejected the word of the LORD, he has also rejected you from being king."

2. Obedience to Jesus' commands.

    a. John 14:15 - 15 **If you love me, you will keep my commandments**.

    b. John 15:13-17 - 13 Greater love has no one than this, that someone lay down his life for his friends. 14 **You are my friends if you do what I command you**. 15 No longer do I call you servants, for the servant does not know what his master is doing; but I have called you friends, for all that I have heard from my Father I have made known to you. 16 You did not choose me, but **I chose you and appointed you that you should go and bear fruit and that your fruit should abide**, so that whatever you ask the Father in my name, he may give it to you. 17 **These things I command you, so that you will love one another**.

    c. Example: The wise and foolish builders. We must not only HEAR the teachings of Jesus, we must DO them.
        i. Matthew 7:24-27 - 24 "Everyone then who **hears these words of mine and does them** will be like a wise man who built his house on the rock. 25 And the rain fell, and the floods came, and the winds blew and beat on that house, but it did not fall, because it had been founded on the rock. 26 And everyone who **hears these words of mine and does not do them** will be like a foolish man who built his house on the sand. 27 And the rain fell, and the floods came, and the winds blew and beat against that house, and it fell, and great was the fall of it."

    d. Evaluate your obedience to the commands and teachings of Jesus. www.manifestinternational.com/free

    Or click the image to download.

3. Obedience to Jesus' voice.

    Obedient: Greek-G5255: *hypekoos*: 1. Giving ear. Obedient.

    Obey: Hebrew-H8085: *sama*: 1. Hear, listen to, obey. Perceive by the ear. 2. Listen and give heed to. 3. Listen, yield to.

    a. John 10:3b-5 - 3b **The sheep hear his voice**, and he calls his own sheep by name and leads them out. 4 When he has brought out all his own, he goes before them, and **the sheep follow him, for they know his voice**. 5 A stranger they will not follow, but they will flee from him, for they do not know the voice of strangers."

    b. John 14:16-18 - 16 And **I will ask the Father, and he will give you another Helper**, to be with you forever, 17 **even the Spirit of truth**, whom the world cannot receive, because it neither sees him nor knows him. You know him, for **he dwells with you and will be in you**. 18 "I will not leave you as orphans; I will come to you.

    c. John 16:12-13 - 12 "I still have many things to say to you, but you cannot bear them now. 13 When the Spirit of truth comes, **he will guide you into all the truth, for he will not speak on his own authority, but whatever he hears he will speak**, and he will declare to you the things that are to come.

d. This fulfills the promise of Isaiah 30:21: - 21 And your ears shall hear a word behind you, saying, "**This is the way, walk in it**," when you turn to the right or when you turn to the left.

e. Be sensitive to the checks and promptings of the Holy Spirit who dwells in you to guide you onto God's path for you and away from paths He does not want for you.

4. Living and walking by the Spirit and not by the flesh.

    a. Romans 8:12-14 - 12 So then, brothers, we are debtors, not to the flesh, to live according to the flesh. 13 For if you live according to the flesh you will die, but **if by the Spirit you put to death the deeds of the body, you will live.** 14 **For all who are led by the Spirit of God are sons of God.**

    b. Galatians 5:16-18 - 16 But I say, **walk by the Spirit, and you will not gratify the desires of the flesh**. 17 For the desires of the flesh are against the Spirit, and the desires of the Spirit are against the flesh, for **these are opposed to each other, to keep you from doing the things you want to do**. 18 But if you are led by the Spirit, you are not under the law.
        i. Galatians 5:22-23 - 22 **But the fruit of the Spirit is** love, joy, peace, patience, kindness, goodness, faithfulness, 23 gentleness, self-control; against such things there is no law.

    c. Example: Jesus.
        i. Jesus did ONLY what He saw the Father doing, said ONLY what the Father told Him to say, and taught ONLY what the Father told Him to teach. He was obedient to the point of death.
        ii. Jesus IS our example of the perfect life lived by the indwelling Holy Spirit. He was born by the power of the Holy Spirit from the womb. We are born again by the power of the Holy Spirit as we walk by the Spirit and allow God to transform us to Christ's likeness.
        iii. Note: Jesus was so submitted under God's authority that a Gentile Centurion recognized Jesus as being under a power higher than Himself.

5. Persevering in keeping our heart tender to God's voice and promptings until Jesus returns.

    a. Example: The recipients of the Letter to the Hebrews.
        i. After many years of persecution and unmet expectations of Jesus' imminent return, they were weary in the faith and beginning to question their salvation in Jesus.
        ii. When they put their faith in Jesus as their Messiah, they had been expelled from their people, and cut off from families, friends, and natural inheritances. But by the time the letter of Hebrews was written, much time had passed.
        iii. They were tempted to return to Judaism which would constitute falling away from the faith, returning to the Old Covenant from the New Covenant.
        iv. Out of the weariness of constant trials and challenges, their hearts had grown dull.

    b. Hebrews 3:7-15 - 7 Therefore, as the Holy Spirit says, "**Today, if you hear his voice**, 8 **do not harden your hearts as in the rebellion, on the day of testing in the wilderness**, 9 where your fathers put me to the test and saw my works for forty years. 10 Therefore I was provoked with that generation, and said, 'They always go astray in their heart; they have not known my ways.' 11 As I swore in my wrath, 'They shall not enter my rest.'" 12 **Take care, brothers, lest there be in any of you an evil, unbelieving heart, leading you to fall away from the living God.** 13 But exhort one another every day, **as long as it is called "today," that none of you may be hardened by the deceitfulness of sin**. 14 For we have come to share in Christ, if

indeed we hold our original confidence firm to the end. 15 As it is said, "**Today, if you hear his voice, do not harden your hearts as in the rebellion.**"
- i. The rebellion was at the waters of Meribah when Israel failed to believe that God was able to provide water in the desert wasteland wilderness. They tested God through unbelief by saying, "Is the Lord among us or not?"
- ii. See also Psalm 78 for a retelling or Israel's constant testing of the Lord through unbelief and hardening their hearts in disobedience to His voice.

c. We must not harden our hearts by ignoring the promptings, checks, and guidance of the Holy Spirit. The Holy Spirit is Christ in us, the hope of glory – God inside of us guiding us from within so that we do not remain in sin, continue in sin, or return to sin. The more we reject the promptings of the Holy Spirit, the harder our heart becomes. This makes us vulnerable to rejecting Jesus and falling away from the faith.

d. Example: Pharoah (See Exodus 7-12.)
- i. Pharaoh's heart was hard.
    - 01. Note: NIV translates it as his heart was "unyielding."
- ii. Pharaoh hardened his heart to the requests of the Lord.
- iii. Then, the Lord hardened Pharaoh's heart and turned him over to destruction.

e. Example: Pharisees (Mark 3:4-6.)
- i. Pharisees' hearts were hardened through religion, legalism, and traditions of men.
- ii. Their hardness of heart angered Jesus and caused them to want to kill Him.

F. On Your Face & Laying Prostrate Before the Lord

1. Laying prostrate is bowing before someone as a sign of reverence, worship, subjection, lowliness, unworthiness, and petition.

> Worship: Hebrew-H7812: *saha*: 1. To bow down. 2. To prostrate oneself before a superior in homage, before royalty or before God in worship. 3. To humbly beseech. 4. To do reverence, do homage, submit oneself.
>
> Prostrate: (v.) To lay oneself flat on the ground face downward, especially in reverence or submission. (adj.) Lying stretched out on the ground with one's face downward. (Dictionary.com.)

a. Subjects bow themselves before kings and royalty.
- i. Lowering oneself before someone is a sign of their "high-ness."
- ii. It shows the ruler's dignity, honor, and exalted rank above the one bowing down.
- iii. The lower the subjects bow, the deeper the reverence they show.

b. Laying prostrate is the ultimate self-humbling and offering of total submission/subservience.

2. If we really understand who God is, we will prostrate ourselves before Him.

a. We deserve the judgment and wrath of God. We deserve penalty and punishment for all of our sin and the sins we commit daily. It is only because of the mercy of God that we are not destroyed. It is only through the shed blood of Jesus that we can be forgiven and continue on in life as if we had never sinned.

i. If we truly understand this, we will fall on our faces out of repentance and reverence.
ii. If we truly appreciate this, we will fall on our faces out of thankfulness and worship.

b. God is all-powerful, all-knowing, totally sovereign over all things. God has everything we could ever possibly need for life and thriving including wisdom, provision, protection, healing, deliverance, etc.
  i. If we truly understand this, we will fall on our faces out of reverence and petition.
  ii. If we truly appreciate this, we will fall on our faces out of thankfulness and worship.

3. Jesus prayed to God on His face. He was heard because of His reverence to God.

  a. Matthew 26:36-39 - 36 Then Jesus went with them to a place called Gethsemane, and he said to his disciples, "Sit here, while I go over there and pray." 37 And taking with him Peter and the two sons of Zebedee, he began to be sorrowful and troubled. 38 Then he said to them, "My soul is very sorrowful, even to death; remain here, and watch with me." 39 And going a little farther **he fell on his face and prayed, saying, "My Father, if it be possible, let this cup pass from me; nevertheless, not as I will, but as you will."**

  b. Hebrews 5:7 - 7 In the days of his flesh, **Jesus offered up prayers and supplications, with loud cries and tears,** to him who was able to save him from death, and **he was heard because of his reverence**.

4. People fell on their faces before God out of reverence, subjection, worship, and to seek His mercy and help.

  a. Example: Abraham had already waited twenty-four years for God to fulfill His promise. But Abraham was not defiant, questioning, or demanding of God in any way. He knew His place before God. When God told Abraham that he would have a miraculous son, Abraham bowed down and rejoiced in thankfulness before the Lord.
    i. Genesis 17:1-3 - 1 When Abram was ninety-nine years old the LORD appeared to Abram and said to him, "I am God Almighty; walk before me, and be blameless, 2 that I may make my covenant between me and you, and may multiply you greatly." 3 **Then Abram fell on his face**.
      01. In acknowledgement of God's power and authority.
    ii. Genesis 17:17 - 17 Then **Abraham fell on his face and laughed** and said to himself, "Shall a child be born to a man who is a hundred years old? Shall Sarah, who is ninety years old, bear a child?"
      01. In thankfulness of God's promise.

  b. Example: Moses. At the Golden Calf incident, the Lord was ready to destroy Israel, but Moses sought the Lord for mercy for His people. Again later, Moses sought the mercy of God.
    i. Deuteronomy 9:18 - 18 Then **I lay prostrate before the LORD** as before, forty days and forty nights. I neither ate bread nor drank water, because of all the sin that you had committed, in doing what was evil in the sight of the LORD to provoke him to anger.
      01. This was after the Golden Calf incident. God was ready to destroy the people but Moses interceded.
    ii. Deuteronomy 9:25-26 - 25 "So **I lay prostrate before the LORD** for these forty days and forty nights, because the LORD had said he would destroy you. 26 And I prayed to the LORD, 'O Lord GOD, do not destroy your people and your heritage, whom you have redeemed through your greatness, whom you have brought out of Egypt with a mighty hand.

01. This was after the people believed the bad report of the spies and did not believe that God could give them the Promised Land. God was ready to destroy the people but Moses interceded.

c. Example: Joshua: The commander of the army of the Lord of Hosts appeared to Joshua. Later, after being defeated at Ai, Joshua and the elders of Israel sought the mercy of God.
  i. Joshua 5:13-15 - 13 When Joshua was by Jericho, he lifted up his eyes and looked, and behold, a man was standing before him with his drawn sword in his hand. And Joshua went to him and said to him, "Are you for us, or for our adversaries?" 14 And he said, "No; but I am the commander of the army of the LORD. Now I have come." And **Joshua fell on his face to the earth and worshiped** and said to him, "What does my lord say to his servant?" 15 And the commander of the LORD's army said to Joshua, "Take off your sandals from your feet, for the place where you are standing is holy." And Joshua did so.
    01. This was before the Israelites entered into their first battle in the Promised Land.
  ii. Joshua 7:6 - 6 Then Joshua tore his clothes and **fell to the earth on his face before the ark of the LORD until the evening, he and the elders of Israel**. And they put dust on their heads.
    01. This was after the first defeat in battle at Ai, due to Achan's disobedience.

d. Example: David: When the angel of the Lord was ready to destroy Jerusalem, David and the elders of Israel fell on their faces before God to seek His mercy.
  i. 1 Chronicles 21:16-17 - 16 And David lifted his eyes and saw the angel of the LORD standing between earth and heaven, and in his hand a drawn sword stretched out over Jerusalem. Then **David and the elders, clothed in sackcloth, fell upon their faces**. 17 And David said to God, "Was it not I who gave command to number the people? It is I who have sinned and done great evil. But these sheep, what have they done? Please let your hand, O LORD my God, be against me and against my father's house. But do not let the plague be on your people."

e. Example: Elijah: By God's word, Elijah had commanded there to be no rain in Israel but the time had come for rain. So Elijah prayed.
  i. 1 Kings 18:42-44 - 42 So Ahab went up to eat and to drink. And Elijah went up to the top of Mount Carmel. And **he bowed himself down on the earth and put his face between his knees**. 43 And he said to his servant, "Go up now, look toward the sea." And he went up and looked and said, "There is nothing." And he said, "Go again," seven times. 44 And at the seventh time he said, "Behold, a little cloud like a man's hand is rising from the sea." And he said, "Go up, say to Ahab, 'Prepare your chariot and go down, lest the rain stop you.'"
  ii. James 5:16b-18 - 16 The prayer of a righteous person has great power as it is working. 17 **Elijah was a man with a nature like ours, and he prayed fervently** that it might not rain, and for three years and six months it did not rain on the earth. 18 Then he prayed again, and heaven gave rain, and the earth bore its fruit.

f. Example: Jehoshaphat & all Judah: Under threat of attack by the combined forces of several enemy nations, Jehoshaphat called for fasting and prayer. The Spirit of the Lord gave a prophetic word of victory and the people worshipped God.
  i. 2 Chronicles 20:15-18 - 15 And he said, "Listen, all Judah and inhabitants of Jerusalem and King Jehoshaphat: Thus says the LORD to you, 'Do not be afraid and do not be dismayed at this great horde, for the battle is not yours but God's. 16 Tomorrow go

down against them. Behold, they will come up by the ascent of Ziz. You will find them at the end of the valley, east of the wilderness of Jeruel. 17 You will not need to fight in this battle. Stand firm, hold your position, and see the salvation of the LORD on your behalf, O Judah and Jerusalem.' Do not be afraid and do not be dismayed. Tomorrow go out against them, and the LORD will be with you." 18 Then **Jehoshaphat bowed his head with his face to the ground, and all Judah and the inhabitants of Jerusalem fell down before the LORD, worshiping the LORD.**

    g. Example: The leper seeking healing from Jesus.
        i. Luke 5:12-13 - 12 While he was in one of the cities, there came a man full of leprosy. And **when he saw Jesus, he fell on his face and begged him, "Lord, if you will, you can make me clean.**" 13 And Jesus stretched out his hand and touched him, saying, "I will; be clean." And immediately the leprosy left him.

5. People fall on their faces at revelation of the glory of God.

    a. When the glory of God was revealed at the Tabernacle and the Temple.
        i. Leviticus 9:23-24 - 23 And Moses and Aaron went into the tent of meeting, and when they came out they blessed the people, and the **glory of the LORD appeared to all** the people. 24 And **fire came out from before the LORD** and consumed the burnt offering and the pieces of fat on the altar, and **when all the people saw it, they shouted and fell on their faces.**
        ii. 2 Chronicles 7:1-3 - 1 As soon as Solomon finished his prayer, **fire came down from heaven** and consumed the burnt offering and the sacrifices, and **the glory of the LORD filled the temple.** 2 And the priests could not enter the house of the LORD, because **the glory of the LORD filled the LORD's house.** 3 When all the people of Israel saw the fire come down and **the glory of the LORD on the temple, they bowed down with their faces to the ground on the pavement and worshiped and gave thanks to the LORD**, saying, "For he is good, for his steadfast love endures forever."
        iii. 1 Kings 8:10-11 - 10 And when the priests came out of the Holy Place, a cloud filled the house of the LORD, 11 **so that the priests could not stand to minister because of the cloud, for the glory of the LORD filled the house of the LORD.**

    b. When fire from heaven answered Elijah's prayer for fire.
        i. 1 Kings 18:38-39 - 38 Then the fire of the LORD fell and consumed the burnt offering and the wood and the stones and the dust, and licked up the water that was in the trench. 39 And when all the people saw it, **they fell on their faces and said, "The LORD, he is God; the LORD, he is God."**

    c. When Ezekiel had visions of the glory of the Lord and of the new Temple in Jerusalem.
        i. Ezekiel 1:27-28 - 27 And upward from what had the appearance of his waist I saw as it were gleaming metal, like the appearance of fire enclosed all around. And downward from what had the appearance of his waist I saw as it were the appearance of fire, and there was brightness around him. 28 Like the appearance of the bow that is in the cloud on the day of rain, so was the appearance of the brightness all around. Such was the appearance of **the likeness of the glory of the LORD. And when I saw it, I fell on my face**, and I heard the voice of one speaking.
        ii. Ezekiel 44:4 - 4 Then he brought me by way of the north gate to the front of the temple, and I looked, and behold, **the glory of the LORD filled the temple** of the LORD. **And I fell on my face.**

- d. When disciples witnessed the transfiguration of Jesus with Moses and Elijah.
    - i. Matthew 17:5-6 - 5 He was still speaking when, behold, **a bright cloud overshadowed them**, and a voice from the cloud said, "This is my beloved Son, with whom I am well pleased; listen to him." 6 When the disciples heard this, **they fell on their faces and were terrified**.
- e. Roman soldiers were overpowered by the glory of the Lord in Gethsemane.
    - i. John 18:6 - 6 When Jesus said to them, "I am he," **they drew back and fell to the ground.**
- f. John at Patmos had a vision and revelation of Jesus.
    - i. Revelation 1:17-18 - 17 When I saw him, **I fell at his feet as though dead**. But he laid his right hand on me, saying, "Fear not, I am the first and the last, 18 and the living one. I died, and behold I am alive forevermore, and I have the keys of Death and Hades.
- g. Sinners fall on their face at the discovery of God among prophetic believers.
    - i. 1 Corinthians 14:24-25 - 24 But if all prophesy, and an unbeliever or outsider enters, he is convicted by all, he is called to account by all, 25 **the secrets of his heart are disclosed, and so, falling on his face, he will worship God** and declare that God is really among you.
- h. Even Dagon the Philistine god had to bow in the presence of the Lord.
    - i. 1 Samuel 5:2-4 - 2 Then the Philistines took the ark of God and brought it into the house of Dagon and set it up beside Dagon. 3 And when the people of Ashdod rose early the next day, behold, **Dagon had fallen face downward on the ground before the ark of the LORD**. So they took Dagon and put him back in his place. 4 But when they rose early on the next morning, behold, **Dagon had fallen face downward on the ground before the ark of the LORD, and the head of Dagon and both his hands were lying cut off** on the threshold. Only the trunk of Dagon was left to him.

6. All creatures of heaven fall on their faces to worship God, acknowledging His glory, worthiness, power, righteousness, and justice.

    - a. Revelation 7:9-12 - 9 After this I looked, and behold, **a great multitude that no one could number, from every nation, from all tribes and peoples and languages, standing before the throne and before the Lamb**, clothed in white robes, with palm branches in their hands, 10 and crying out with a loud voice, "Salvation belongs to our God who sits on the throne, and to the Lamb!" 11 And **all the angels were standing around the throne and around the elders and the four living creatures, and they fell on their faces before the throne and worshiped God**, 12 saying, "Amen! Blessing and glory and wisdom and thanksgiving and honor and power and might be to our God forever and ever! Amen."
        - i. Everyone in heaven is on their face before the Lamb of God.

    - b. Revelation 11:16-18 - 16 **And the twenty-four elders who sit on their thrones before God fell on their faces and worshiped God**, 17 saying, "We give thanks to you, Lord God Almighty, who is and who was, for you have taken your great power and begun to reign. 18 The nations raged, but your wrath came, and the time for the dead to be judged, and for rewarding your servants, the prophets and saints, and those who fear your name, both small and great, and for destroying the destroyers of the earth."

    - c. God's sovereign rule over all the nations of the earth and the righteousness of His judgments is cause for great and deep worship.

Unit Five: Humble Yourself Before God, Part Two: Seeking

> You have said, "Seek my face." My heart says to you, "Your face, LORD, do I seek."
>
> Psalm 27:8

A. Prayer

1. Prayer is simply communicating with God. It demonstrates that we value God for who He is and the significance of His sovereignty. It reveals our faith in who He is.

    a. Hebrews 11:6 - 6 And without faith it is impossible to please him, for **whoever would draw near to God must believe that he exists** and that he rewards those who seek him.

    > Draw Near: Greek-G4334: *proserchomai*: 1. Come. 2. Come to. 3. Draw near to. 4. Ascend to. From root words which mean approach, visit, go towards, or follow.
    > *Used in Hebrews 4:16, 7:25, 10:1&22, 11:6, 12:18&22.*

    > Draw Near: Greek-G1448: *engizo*: 1. To bring near. 2. To join one thing to another. 3. To draw or come near to. 4. To approach.
    > *Used in James 4:8; Hebrews 7:19.*

2. Because of the righteousness of Jesus, we can be confident that God hears our prayer and will answer us. The God of all creation delights to hear us talk to Him.

    a. We can go boldly before God to ask for His help.
        i. Hebrews 4:16 - 16 **Let us then with confidence draw near to the throne of grace**, that we may receive mercy and find grace to **help in time of need**.

    b. We can be confident that God hears us because by faith in Jesus, we are righteous.
        i. 1 John 5:14-15 - 14 And this is the confidence that we have toward him, **that if we ask anything according to his will he hears us**. 15 And if we know that **he hears us in whatever we ask**, we know that we have the requests that we have asked of him.
        ii. Proverbs 15:29 - 29 The LORD is far from the wicked, but **he hears the prayer of the righteous**.
        iii. Psalm 34:17 - 17 **When the righteous cry for help, the LORD hears** and delivers them out of all their troubles.

3. We can talk to God about anything and everything. God wants us to pour our hearts out to Him. We can bring Him our questions, concerns and anxieties. We can ask God for anything.

    a. We can pour our hearts out to the Lord.
        i. Psalm 62:8 - 8 Trust in him at all times, O people; **pour out your heart before him**; God is a refuge for us. Selah

ii. Psalm 102:1-2 - 1 **A Prayer of one afflicted, when he is faint and pours out his complaint before the LORD.** Hear my prayer, O LORD; let my cry come to you! 2 Do not hide your face from me in the day of my distress! Incline your ear to me; answer me speedily in the day when I call!
iii. Psalm 142:1-2 - 1 A Maskil of David, when he was in the cave. A Prayer. With my voice **I cry out to the LORD**; with my voice I plead for mercy to the LORD. 2 **I pour out my complaint before him; I tell my trouble before him.**
iv. Psalm 42:2-5 - 2 My soul thirsts for God, for the living God. When shall I come and appear before God? 3 My tears have been my food day and night, while they say to me all the day long, "Where is your God?" 4 These things I remember, **as I pour out my soul**: how I would go with the throng and lead them in procession to the house of God with glad shouts and songs of praise, a multitude keeping festival. 5 Why are you cast down, O my soul, and why are you in turmoil within me? **Hope in God**; for I shall again praise him, my salvation

b. We can bring our concerns to God and trust Him to help us and give us His peace.
   i. Philippians 4:6-7 - 6 **do not be anxious about anything, but in everything by prayer and supplication with thanksgiving let your requests be made known to God.** 7 And the peace of God, which surpasses all understanding, will guard your hearts and your minds in Christ Jesus.
   ii. 1 Peter 5:6-7 - 6 Humble yourselves, therefore, under the mighty hand of God so that at the proper time he may exalt you, 7 **casting all your anxieties on him, because he cares for you**.

c. We can ask God for anything.
   i. John 15:7 - 7 If you abide in me, and my words abide in you, **ask whatever you wish, and it will be done for you**.
   ii. John 14:13-14 - 13 **Whatever you ask in my name, this I will do**, that the Father may be glorified in the Son. 14 **If you ask me anything in my name, I will do it.**

B. Calling Upon & Inquiring of the Lord

1. Calling upon His name is what God desires from us as our demonstration of faith and humbling ourselves to ask for His help.

   > Call: Hebrew-H7121: qa'ra: 1. To call, call out, recite, cry out. 2. To call, cry, utter a loud sound. Almost identical with H7122: qara: To meet, accost, or encounter, whether accidentally or in a hostile manner.

   a. After Adam and Eve had been banished from Eden and Cain had been cursed to wander the earth, Enosh longed for restoration with God so he called out to Him.
      i. Genesis 4:26 - 26 To Seth also a son was born, and he called his name Enosh. **At that time people began to call upon the name of the LORD.**

   b. God desires for us to call upon Him more than He desires sacrifice. He wants relationship not religious obligation.
      i. Psalm 50:14-15 - 14 Offer to God a sacrifice of thanksgiving, and perform your vows to the Most High, 15 and **call upon me in the day of trouble; I will deliver you, and you shall glorify me."**

c. David lived a life of calling upon the name of the Lord. He was a man after God's heart.
   i. Psalm 17:6-9 - 6 **I call upon you**, for you will answer me, O God; **incline your ear to me; hear my words**. 7 Wondrously show your steadfast love, O Savior of those who seek refuge from their adversaries at your right hand. 8 Keep me as the apple of your eye; hide me in the shadow of your wings, 9 from the wicked who do me violence, my deadly enemies who surround me.
   ii. Psalm 18:3, 6 - 3 **I call upon the LORD, who is worthy to be praised**, and I am saved from my enemies. ... 6 **In my distress I called upon the LORD; to my God I cried for help**. From his temple he heard my voice, and my cry to him reached his ears.
   iii. Psalm 27:7 - 7 **Hear, O LORD, when I cry aloud**; be gracious to me and answer me!
   iv. Psalm 86:5 - 5 For you, O Lord, are good and forgiving, **abounding in steadfast love to all who call upon you**.

2. We inquire of the Lord and ask for His counsel to Him so that we can do His will rather than what seems right in our own eyes.

   > Inquire: Hebrew-H7592: sa'al: 1. To ask, inquire, borrow, or beg. 2. To enquire. To practice beggary. 3. To request, consult, ask counsel on.

   a. David constantly inquired of the Lord. God gave Him success and called Him a man after His own heart who will do all His will.
      i. 1 Samuel 23:1-4 - 1 Now they told David, "Behold, the Philistines are fighting against Keilah and are robbing the threshing floors." 2 **Therefore David inquired of the LORD**, "Shall I go and attack these Philistines?" And the LORD said to David, "Go and attack the Philistines and save Keilah." But David's men said to him, "Behold, we are afraid here in Judah; how much more then if we go to Keilah against the armies of the Philistines?" 4 Then **David inquired of the LORD again**. And the LORD answered him, "Arise, go down to Keilah, for I will give the Philistines into your hand."
      ii. 1 Samuel 23:9-12 - 9 David knew that Saul was plotting harm against him. And he said to Abiathar the priest, "Bring the ephod here." 10 Then **David said, "O LORD, the God of Israel**, your servant has surely heard that Saul seeks to come to Keilah, to destroy the city on my account. 11 Will the men of Keilah surrender me into his hand? Will Saul come down, as your servant has heard? **O LORD, the God of Israel, please tell your servant**." And the LORD said, "He will come down." 12 **Then David said**, "Will the men of Keilah surrender me and my men into the hand of Saul?" And the LORD said, "They will surrender you."
      iii. 1 Samuel 30:6-8 - 6 And David was greatly distressed, for the people spoke of stoning him, because all the people were bitter in soul, each for his sons and daughters. But **David strengthened himself in the LORD his God**. 7 And David said to Abiathar the priest, the son of Ahimelech, "Bring me the ephod." So Abiathar brought the ephod to David. 8 And **David inquired of the LORD**, "Shall I pursue after this band? Shall I overtake them?" He answered him, "Pursue, for you shall surely overtake and shall surely rescue."
      iv. 2 Samuel 2:1 - 1 After this [the death of Saul] **David inquired of the LORD**, "Shall I go up into any of the cities of Judah?" And the LORD said to him, "Go up." David said, "To which shall I go up?" And he said, "To Hebron."
      v. 2 Samuel 5:17-19, 22-24 - 17 When the Philistines heard that David had been anointed king over Israel, all the Philistines went up to search for David. But David heard of it and went down to the stronghold. 18 Now the Philistines had come and spread out in the Valley of Rephaim. 19 And **David inquired of the LORD**, "Shall I go up against the Philistines? Will you give them into my hand?" And the LORD said to David, "Go up, for I will certainly give the Philistines into your hand." ... 22 And the Philistines came up yet

again and spread out in the Valley of Rephaim. 23 And when **David inquired of the LORD**, he said, "You shall not go up; go around to their rear, and come against them opposite the balsam trees. 24 And when you hear the sound of marching in the tops of the balsam trees, then rouse yourself, for then the LORD has gone out before you to strike down the army of the Philistines."
   vi. Acts 13:22 - 22 And when he had removed him, he raised up David to be their king, of whom he testified and said, '**I have found in David the son of Jesse a man after my heart, who will do all my will**.'

3. Failure to inquire of the Lord has led to unfortunate consequences.

   a. Joshua 9:14-15 - 14 So the men took some of their provisions, **but did not ask counsel from the LORD**. 15 And Joshua made peace with them and made a covenant with them, to let them live, and the leaders of the congregation swore to them.
      i. This led to an alliance between Israel and the Gibeonites whom God had commanded them to destroy out of the land.

   b. 1 Chronicles 10:13-14 - 13 So Saul died for his breach of faith. He broke faith with the LORD in that he did not keep the command of the LORD, and also consulted a medium, seeking guidance. 14 **He did not seek guidance from the LORD**. Therefore the LORD put him to death and turned the kingdom over to David the son of Jesse.
      i. Saul did not seek the Lord and instead inquired of mediums.

   c. 1 Chronicles 15:13 - 13 Because you did not carry it the first time, the LORD our God broke out against us, **because we did not seek him according to the rule**."
      i. Uzzah had been killed for stretching out his hand to the Ark of God when it was being transported on a cart.

4. If God does not seem to answer or does not give us what we asked for, it may be because we have asked with the wrong motives or for the wrong reasons. The righteousness of God through faith in Jesus, and using Jesus' name in prayer is not a free pass for worldliness and fleshly requests. We must remain humble before God in prayer.

   a. James 4:3-10 - 3 **You ask and do not receive, because you ask wrongly, to spend it on your passions**. 4 You adulterous people! Do you not know that friendship with the world is enmity with God? Therefore whoever wishes to be a friend of the world makes himself an enemy of God. 5 Or do you suppose it is to no purpose that the Scripture says, "He yearns jealously over the spirit that he has made to dwell in us"? 6 But he gives more grace. Therefore it says, "God opposes the proud but gives grace to the humble." 7 **Submit yourselves therefore to God.** Resist the devil, and he will flee from you. 8 **Draw near to God, and he will draw near to you. Cleanse your hands, you sinners, and purify your hearts, you double-minded**. 9 Be wretched and mourn and weep. Let your laughter be turned to mourning and your joy to gloom. 10 **Humble yourselves before the Lord, and he will exalt you.**

> Submit: Greek-G5293: hypotasso: 1. Arrange under, to subordinate. 2. To subject one's self, obey. 3. To submit to one's control. 4. To yield to one's admonition or advice. *This word was a Greek military term meaning "to arrange [troop divisions] in a military fashion under the command of a leader". In non-military use, it was "a voluntary attitude of giving in, cooperating, assuming responsibility, and carrying a burden".*

C. At His Feet

1. At Jesus' feet: the one thing needful. The position of listening.

    a. Mary sitting at Jesus' feet in contrast to Martha busy with serving.
        i. Luke 10:38-42 - 38 Now as they went on their way, Jesus entered a village. And a woman named Martha welcomed him into her house. 39 And she had a sister called **Mary, who sat at the Lord's feet and listened to his teaching**. 40 But Martha was distracted with much serving. And she went up to him and said, "Lord, do you not care that my sister has left me to serve alone? Tell her then to help me." 41 But the Lord answered her, "**Martha, Martha, you are anxious and troubled about many things**, 42 **but one thing is necessary. Mary has chosen the good portion, which will not be taken away from her**."
            01. The KJV and NKJV translate the word necessary as needful.

        <u>Needful</u>: Greek-G5532: *chreia*: 1. Necessity, need. 2. Duty or business. From the root word for employment.

    b. Example: Boy Samuel kept hearing the call of the Lord but thought it was Eli the priest. When he realized it was the Lord, he stilled himself before the Ark of God and listened to what the Lord had to say to Him.
        i. 1 Samuel 3:10 NIV - 10 The LORD came and stood there, calling as at the other times, "Samuel! Samuel!" Then Samuel said, "**Speak, for your servant is listening**."

    c. Note: Even our service for God can distract us from the most important thing. In fact, Labor for the Lord is potentially the biggest distraction from our highest duty of sitting at His feet.
        i. It is more gratifying to the flesh to be active in serving rather than sitting at God's feet. But if God did not author our activity or His Spirit is not in it, it will surely burn in the fires of judgment and we will receive no reward for it. (See 1 Corinthians 3:12-13.)

2. At Jesus' feet: the place of petition.

    a. Jairus asking Jesus to restore his daughter to life.
        i. Matthew 9:18 - 18 While he was saying these things to them, behold, **a ruler came in and knelt before him**, saying, "My daughter has just died, but come and lay your hand on her, and she will live."

    b. The Syrophoenician woman begging Jesus to deliver her daughter from a demon.
        i. Mark 7:25-26 - 25 But immediately **a woman whose little daughter had an unclean spirit heard of him and came and fell down at his feet**. 26 Now the woman was a Gentile, a Syrophoenician by birth. And she begged him to cast the demon out of her daughter.

    c. See on Unit 4, On Your Face

3. At Jesus' feet: the place of gratitude.

    a. A sinful woman thankful for the mercy of God.
        i. Luke 7:36-47 - 36 One of the Pharisees asked him to eat with him, and he went into the Pharisee's house and reclined at table. 37 And behold, a woman of the city, who was a sinner, when she learned that he was reclining at table in the Pharisee's house,

brought an alabaster flask of ointment, 38 and standing behind him **at his feet, weeping, she began to wet his feet with her tears and wiped them with the hair of her head and kissed his feet and anointed them with the ointment**. 39 Now when the Pharisee who had invited him saw this, he said to himself, "If this man were a prophet, he would have known who and what sort of woman this is who is touching him, for she is a sinner." 40 And Jesus answering said to him, "Simon, I have something to say to you." And he answered, "Say it, Teacher." 41 "A certain moneylender had two debtors. One owed five hundred denarii, and the other fifty. 42 When they could not pay, he cancelled the debt of both. Now which of them will love him more?" 43 Simon answered, "The one, I suppose, for whom he cancelled the larger debt." And he said to him, "You have judged rightly." 44 Then turning toward the woman he said to Simon, "**Do you see this woman? I entered your house; you gave me no water for my feet, but she has wet my feet with her tears and wiped them with her hair. 45 You gave me no kiss, but from the time I came in she has not ceased to kiss my feet. 46 You did not anoint my head with oil, but she has anointed my feet with ointment. 47 Therefore I tell you, her sins, which are many, are forgiven--for she loved much**. But he who is forgiven little, loves little."

    b. If we love the Lord and are thankful for all He has done for us, we will not be ashamed to sit as His feet and pour our lives out for Him, even if it costs us everything we have and all we have worked for. He is worthy of everything we have to offer Him.

4. At Jesus' feet: the place of preparation.

    a. Mary prepared Jesus for His crucifixion and burial.
        i. Matthew 26:6-13 - 6 Now when Jesus was at Bethany in the house of Simon the leper, **7 a woman came up to him with an alabaster flask of very expensive ointment, and she poured it on his head as he reclined at table**. 8 And when the disciples saw it, they were indignant, saying, "Why this waste? 9 For this could have been sold for a large sum and given to the poor." 10 But Jesus, aware of this, said to them, "**Why do you trouble the woman? For she has done a beautiful thing to me**. 11 For you always have the poor with you, but you will not always have me. 12 **In pouring this ointment on my body, she has done it to prepare me for burial**. 13 Truly, I say to you, wherever this gospel is proclaimed in the whole world, what she has done will also be told in memory of her." (See also Mark 14:3-9; John 12:1-8.)
            01. Note: John identifies this woman as the same Mary who sat at Jesus' feet.
            02. Note: This is a different woman than the woman who washed Jesus' feet with her tears and anointed His feet with oil.

    b. When God calls us to challenging things, to battles, or to die to ourselves and our own desires, He calls us to sit at His feet. It is there that He prepares us and girds us with His strength and counsel. There, He fills us with Himself.

D. Seek His Face

1. To seek the face of someone, means to seek their presence. It requires deep intimacy to look someone in the face. God wants this type of intimate relationship with each one of us.

<u>Face</u>: Hebrew-H6440: *panim*: 1. Face. 2. Presence of a person. 3. Face or surface. 4. Before or in front of. 5. In the face of or in the presence of.

  a. The Lord wants us to seek His face.
      i. Psalm 27:8-9 - 8 **You have said, "Seek my face**." My heart says to you, "**Your face, LORD, do I seek**." 9 **Hide not your face from me**. Turn not your servant away in anger, O you who have been my help. Cast me not off; forsake me not, O God of my salvation!
      ii. Psalm 105:4 - 4 Seek the LORD and his strength; **seek his presence continually!**

  b. Example: David sought the face of the Lord to inquire about the cause of a three-year famine in the land.
      i. 2 Samuel 21:1 - 1 Now **there was a famine in the days of David for three years**, year after year. And **David sought the face of the LORD**. And the LORD said, "There is bloodguilt on Saul and on his house, because he put the Gibeonites to death."

  c. The Lord shining His face upon us or lifting up His countenance upon us is a sign of His favor and blessing.
      i. Numbers 6:24-26 - 24 The LORD bless you and keep you; 25 **the LORD make his face to shine upon you** and be gracious to you; 26 **the LORD lift up his countenance upon you** and give you peace.

2. Moses spoke to the Lord face to face and his face shone. The Lord spoke to Moses plainly, as a man speaks to His friend, and not in riddles or mysteries, visions, dreams, or omens which needed to be interpreted.

    a. Exodus 33:9, 11a - 9 When Moses entered the tent, the pillar of cloud would descend and stand at the entrance of the tent, and the LORD would speak with Moses. ... 11 Thus the **LORD used to speak to Moses face to face, as a man speaks to his friend**.

    b. Numbers 12:6-8 NIV - 6 he said, "Listen to my words: "**When there is a prophet among you, I, the LORD, reveal myself to them in visions, I speak to them in dreams**. 7 But this is not true of my servant Moses; he is faithful in all my house. 8 **With him I speak face to face, clearly and not in riddles; he sees the form of the LORD**. Why then were you not afraid to speak against my servant Moses?"

    c. Exodus 34:29-30 - 29 When Moses came down from Mount Sinai, with the two tablets of the testimony in his hand as he came down from the mountain, **Moses did not know that the skin of his face shone because he had been talking with God**. 30 Aaron and all the people of Israel saw Moses, and behold, **the skin of his face shone**, and they were afraid to come near him.

3. Because of the righteousness of Jesus, we can behold the glory of the Lord and He will speak to us plainly, as His beloved children. We are transformed by His presence.

    a. 2 Corinthians 3:12-13, 18 - 12 Since we have such a hope, we are very bold, 13 not like Moses, who would put a veil over his face so that the Israelites might not gaze at the outcome of what was being brought to an end. ... 18 **And we all, with unveiled face, beholding the glory of the Lord, are being transformed into the same image from one degree of glory to another**. For this comes from the Lord who is the Spirit.

E. Fasting

1. Fasting is an act of afflicting our bodies and souls to humble ourselves before God by abstaining from food. It is entering into voluntary weakness in our flesh to silence its impulses and increase our dependence on the Holy Spirit.

   a. Note: abstaining from other activities is part of repentance and self-denial but it is not fasting. Biblical fasting is only from food.

      Fast: Hebrew-H6684: *sum*: 1. To abstain from food. 2. To cover or shut the mouth.

      Fasting: Greek-G5532: *nesteuo*: 1. To abstain as a religious exercise from food and drink: either entirely or from customary and choice nourishment.

   b. The Day of Atonement required mandatory fasting for everyone in Israel as an act of self-affliction and humbling themselves before God.
      i. See Leviticus 16, and Leviticus 23:27-32. It is known as the Fast. (Acts 27:9.)
      ii. Note: the work of atoning for sin is God's alone. Only God can grant forgiveness.

   c. Note: God is the one who sustains us and gives us life, even more than food. Fasting acknowledges our need for God more than food.

2. Personal and corporate fasting was done to demonstrate contrition and returning to the Lord and also to seek His pardon and mercy from justifiable destruction due to sin and error.

   a. 1 Samuel 7:3, 6a - 3 And Samuel said to all the house of Israel, "**If you are returning to the LORD with all your heart**, then put away the foreign gods and the Ashtaroth from among you and direct your heart to the LORD and serve him only, and he will deliver you out of the hand of the Philistines." ... 6 So they gathered at Mizpah and **drew water and poured it out before the LORD and fasted on that day and said there, "We have sinned against the LORD."**

   b. Joel 2:12-17 - 12 "Yet even now," declares the LORD, "**return to me with all your heart, with fasting, with weeping, and with mourning**; 13 and **rend your hearts and not your garments**." Return to the LORD your God, for he is gracious and merciful, slow to anger, and abounding in steadfast love; and he relents over disaster. 14 Who knows whether he will not turn and relent, and leave a blessing behind him, a grain offering and a drink offering for the LORD your God? 15 Blow the trumpet in Zion; **consecrate a fast**; call a solemn assembly; 16 gather the people. Consecrate the congregation; assemble the elders; gather the children, even nursing infants. Let the bridegroom leave his room, and the bride her chamber. 17 Between the vestibule and the altar **let the priests, the ministers of the LORD, weep and say, "Spare your people, O LORD, and make not your heritage a reproach, a byword among the nations. Why should they say among the peoples, 'Where is their God?'"**

   c. Daniel 9:3-6 - 3 Then I turned my face to the Lord God, **seeking him by prayer and pleas for mercy with fasting and sackcloth and ashes.** 4 I prayed to the LORD my God and made confession, saying, "O Lord, the great and awesome God, who keeps covenant and steadfast love with those who love him and keep his commandments, 5 **we have sinned and done wrong and acted wickedly and rebelled, turning aside from your commandments and rules.** 6 **We have not listened to your servants the prophets**, who spoke in your name to our kings, our princes, and our fathers, and to all the people of the land.

d. Nehemiah 1:3-11 - 3 And they said to me, "The remnant there in the province who had survived the exile is in great trouble and shame. The wall of Jerusalem is broken down, and its gates are destroyed by fire." 4 As soon as I heard these words **I sat down and wept and mourned for days, and I continued fasting and praying before the God of heaven.** 5 And I said, "O LORD God of heaven, the great and awesome God who keeps covenant and steadfast love with those who love him and keep his commandments, 6 let your ear be attentive and your eyes open, to hear the prayer of your servant that I now pray before you day and night for the people of Israel your servants, confessing the sins of the people of Israel, which we have sinned against you. Even I and my father's house have sinned. 7 **We have acted very corruptly against you and have not kept the commandments, the statutes, and the rules that you commanded your servant Moses.** 8 Remember the word that you commanded your servant Moses, saying, 'If you are unfaithful, I will scatter you among the peoples, 9 but if you return to me and keep my commandments and do them, though your outcasts are in the uttermost parts of heaven, from there I will gather them and bring them to the place that I have chosen, to make my name dwell there.' 10 They are your servants and your people, whom you have redeemed by your great power and by your strong hand. 11 **O Lord, let your ear be attentive to the prayer of your servant, and to the prayer of your servants who delight to fear your name, and give success to your servant today, and grant him mercy in the sight of this man.**" Now I was cupbearer to the king.

3. Fasting is a way of seeking the Lord for mercy, protection, victory, or direction.

    a. 2 Chronicles 20:2-4 - 2 Some men came and told Jehoshaphat, "A great multitude is coming against you from Edom, from beyond the sea; and, behold, they are in Hazazon-tamar" (that is, Engedi). 3 Then Jehoshaphat was afraid and **set his face to seek the LORD, and proclaimed a fast throughout all Judah.** 4 And Judah assembled **to seek help from the LORD;** from all the cities of Judah they came to seek the LORD.

    b. Ezra 8:21-23 - 21 Then **I proclaimed a fast** there, at the river Ahava, **that we might humble ourselves before our God, to seek from him a safe journey for ourselves, our children, and all our goods.** 22 For I was ashamed to ask the king for a band of soldiers and horsemen to protect us against the enemy on our way, since we had told the king, "The hand of our God is for good on all who seek him, and the power of his wrath is against all who forsake him." 23 **So we fasted and implored our God for this**, and he listened to our entreaty.

    c. Esther 4:15-16 - 15 Then Esther told them to reply to Mordecai, 16 "**Go, gather all the Jews to be found in Susa, and hold a fast on my behalf, and do not eat or drink for three days, night or day.** I and my young women will also fast as you do. Then I will go to the king, though it is against the law, and if I perish, I perish."

4. Fasting is a way of seeking the Lord for mercy for the sick, for their healing and deliverance.

    a. Psalm 35:13-14 - 13 But I, **when they were sick**-- I wore sackcloth; **I afflicted myself with fasting**; I prayed with head bowed on my chest. 14 I went about as though I grieved for my friend or my brother; as one who laments his mother, **I bowed down in mourning.**

    b. 2 Samuel 12:16-23 - 16 David therefore sought God on behalf of the child. And **David fasted and went in and lay all night on the ground.** 17 And the elders of his house stood beside him, to raise him from the ground, but he would not, **nor did he eat food with them.** 18 On the seventh day the child died. And the servants of David were afraid to tell him that the child was dead, for they said, "Behold, while the child was yet alive, we spoke to him, and he did

not listen to us. How then can we say to him the child is dead? He may do himself some harm." 19 But when David saw that his servants were whispering together, David understood that the child was dead. And David said to his servants, **"Is the child dead?" They said, "He is dead."** 20 Then David arose from the earth and washed and anointed himself and changed his clothes. And he went into the house of the LORD and worshiped. He then went to his own house. **And when he asked, they set food before him, and he ate**. 21 Then his servants said to him, "What is this thing that you have done? **You fasted and wept for the child while he was alive; but when the child died, you arose and ate food**." 22 He said, "**While the child was still alive, I fasted and wept, for I said, 'Who knows whether the LORD will be gracious to me, that the child may live?**' 23 But now he is dead. Why should I fast? Can I bring him back again? I shall go to him, but he will not return to me."
    i. Note: Fasting does not guarantee the results we petition for. It is an act of humility, not a method of twisting God's arm.
    ii. Note: David fasted to petition the Lord for mercy for the life of the child. The death of the child revealed God's decision. Therefore, David stopped fasting and though sorrowful, was at peace with God's will.

  c. Mark 9:28-29 NKJV - 28 And when He had come into the house, His disciples asked Him privately, "Why could we not cast it out?" 29 So He said to them, "**This kind [of demon] can come out by nothing but prayer and fasting**."
    i. Fasting is the deepest way to humble oneself and repent before the Lord to seek His mercy.
    ii. Note: In the Matthew version of this, Jesus may be referring to the unbelief of the disciples that could not come out except by fasting. Their flesh and lack of faith was an obstruction. (Matthew 17:14-21)

5. Fasting from luxurious or worldly foods is a way of setting ourselves apart to the Lord.

  a. Daniel 1:5, 8, 11-12 - 5 **The king assigned them a daily portion of the food that the king ate, and of the wine that he drank**. They were to be educated for three years, and at the end of that time they were to stand before the king. ... 8 **But Daniel resolved that he would not defile himself with the king's food, or with the wine that he drank**. Therefore he asked the chief of the eunuchs to allow him not to defile himself. ... 11 Then Daniel said to the steward whom the chief of the eunuchs had assigned over Daniel, Hananiah, Mishael, and Azariah, 12 "Test your servants for ten days; **let us be given vegetables to eat and water to drink**.
    i. Note 1: Daniel may have been obeying the wisdom of Proverbs 23:1-3 - 1 **When you sit down to eat with a ruler**, observe carefully what is before you, 2 and put a knife to your throat if you are given to appetite. 3 **Do not desire his delicacies, for they are deceptive food.**

  b. Note 2: Daniel did not just eat this way for ten days or twenty-one days. He ate this way for sixty-five years – as long as he was in the Babylonian court. (See Daniel 1:21.)
    i. Daniel 10:2-3 - 2 In those days I, Daniel, was mourning for three weeks. 3 **I ate no delicacies, no meat or wine entered my mouth, nor did I anoint myself at all**, for the full three weeks.
    ii. Note: After Babylon's fall, Daniel returned to a standard diet, including meat.
    iii. The initial Jewish exiles had returned to the Land of Judah but had faced such severe opposition that the work of rebuilding the Temple had stopped. Therefore, Daniel fasted to seek the Lord.

6. People fasted to humble themselves as they awaited the arrival of the Messiah.

a. John the Baptist and his disciples fasted and ate a peculiar diet.
      i. Matthew 3:4 - 4 Now John wore a garment of camel's hair and a leather belt around his waist, and **his food was locusts and wild honey**.
      ii. Luke 5:33 - 33 And they said to him, "**The disciples of John fast often and offer prayers**, and so do the disciples of the Pharisees, but yours eat and drink."

   b. A widow named Anna fasted in expectation.
      i. Luke 2:36-37 - 36 And there was a prophetess, Anna, the daughter of Phanuel, of the tribe of Asher. She was advanced in years, having lived with her husband seven years from when she was a virgin, 37 and then as a widow until she was eighty-four. **She did not depart from the temple, worshiping with fasting and prayer night and day**.

7. Jesus fasted to humble Himself before God before beginning His ministry.

   a. Luke 4:1-2, 14 - 1 And Jesus, full of the Holy Spirit, returned from the Jordan and was led by the Spirit in the wilderness 2 for forty days, being tempted by the devil. And **he ate nothing during those days. And when they were ended, he was hungry**. ... 14 And **Jesus returned in the power of the Spirit** to Galilee, and a report about him went out through all the surrounding country.
      i. When Jesus was most weakened in human strength and susceptible to temptation, the devil came to test Him. He resisted evil in this vulnerable state.
      ii. Jesus fasted before beginning His ministry. Most likely, He was receiving instructions from the Father as to how He was to go about His mission, what He was to do and what He was to teach.
      iii. Jesus came out of fasting in the power of God, having resisted temptation and being empowered by the Spirit of the Lord.

8. Jesus' disciples did not fast while He was with them. But He said that His disciples will fast.

   a. Mark 2:18-20 - 18 Now John's disciples and the Pharisees were fasting. And people came and said to him, "Why do John's disciples and the disciples of the Pharisees fast, **but your disciples do not fast**?" 19 And Jesus said to them, "**Can the wedding guests fast while the bridegroom is with them?** As long as they have the bridegroom with them, **they cannot fast**. 20 The days will come when the bridegroom is taken away from them, and **then they will fast in that day**.
      i. Jesus is the bridegroom. He was celebrating His engagement to the bride and giving out "new garments" of righteousness through faith in Him for the wedding feast.
      ii. When the bridegroom departed to prepare a place for the Bride (Jesus' ascension to heaven) then He said His disciples will fast for His return.

   b. Jesus did not starve people while He was with them. He fed them.
      i. Matthew 15:32 KJV - 32 Then Jesus called his disciples unto him, and said, I have compassion on the multitude, because they continue with me now three days, and have nothing to eat: and **I will not send them away fasting**, lest they faint in the way.

   c. Jesus' disciples did/do fast. Believers in the Book of Acts fasted as an act of worship and seeking God. And they fasted before appointing servants to the work of the Lord.
      i. Acts 13:2-3 - 2 While they were **worshiping the Lord and fasting**, the Holy Spirit said, "Set apart for me Barnabas and Saul for the work to which I have called them." 3 Then **after fasting and praying they laid their hands on them and sent them off**.
      ii. Acts 14:23 - 23 And when they had appointed elders for them in every church, **with prayer and fasting they committed them to the Lord** in whom they had believed.

iii. 2 Corinthians 6:4-5 NKJV - 4 But in all [things] we commend ourselves as ministers of God: in much patience, in tribulations, in needs, in distresses, 5 in stripes, in imprisonments, in tumults, in labors, in sleeplessness, in **fastings**;
- 01. Paul fasted regularly as a minister of God, and more often than others.

d. In the New Covenant as followers of Jesus, we can and should fast for the right reasons to humble ourselves before God and seek His face.
  i. We can still show contrition for our sin.
  ii. We still need to seek the direction, protection, and to grow our faith through resisting the demands and cravings of our flesh to be strengthened in the Spirit of the Lord.

9. Fasting can be done for the wrong reasons.

   a. Israel fasted to be seen by God. Their heart was in it for their own gain and not for the Lord. They were fasting out of religious obligation rather than true mourning for sin.
      i. Isaiah 58:3-4 - 3 **'Why have we fasted, and you see it not?** Why have we humbled ourselves, and you take no knowledge of it?' Behold, **in the day of your fast you seek your own pleasure, and oppress all your workers**. 4 Behold, you fast only to quarrel and to fight and to hit with a wicked fist. **Fasting like yours this day will not make your voice to be heard on high**.
      ii. Zechariah 7:5-6 - 5 "Say to all the people of the land and the priests, **'When you fasted and mourned in the fifth month and in the seventh, for these seventy years, was it for me that you fasted?** 6 And when you eat and when you drink, do you not eat for yourselves and drink for yourselves?
      iii. God is not fooled when we fast for selfish reasons or religious displays.

   b. Hypocrites fast to be seen by men, to be regarded as spiritual people.
      i. Matthew 6:16 - 16 "And when you fast, do not look gloomy like the hypocrites, for **they disfigure their faces that their fasting may be seen by others**. Truly, I say to you, they have received their reward.
      ii. While fasting should not be done to be seen, some people will be impacted by your fasting and need to know about it. The motive of fasting or sharing with others about fasting must not be selfish, religious, or to be regarded by others as a spiritual person.
      iii. If fasting is done with a motive of religious display or self-exaltation, we will receive no heavenly reward for it.

   c. Pharisees' fasting was done from self-righteousness and perpetuated their self-righteousness. The Parable of the Pharisee and Tax Collector.
      i. Luke 18:9-14 - 9 He also told this parable to some **who trusted in themselves that they were righteous, and treated others with contempt**: 10 "Two men went up into the temple to pray, one a Pharisee and the other a tax collector. 11 The Pharisee, standing by himself, prayed thus: 'God, I thank you that I am not like other men, extortioners, unjust, adulterers, or even like this tax collector. 12 **I fast twice a week**; I give tithes of all that I get.' 13 But the tax collector, standing far off, would not even lift up his eyes to heaven, but beat his breast, saying, **'God, be merciful to me, a sinner!'** 14 I tell you, this man went down to his house justified, rather than the other. For everyone who exalts himself will be humbled, but the one who humbles himself will be exalted."

   d. Ascetics fast out of religious ascent, but it is of no value in crucifying the flesh.

- i. Colossians 2:20-23 - 20 If with Christ you died to the elemental spirits of the world, why, as if you were still alive in the world, do you submit to regulations-- 21 "**Do not handle, Do not taste, Do not touch**" 22 (referring to things that all perish as they are used)-- according to human precepts and teachings? 23 These have indeed an **appearance of wisdom in promoting self-made religion and asceticism and severity to the body**, but they are of no value in stopping the indulgence of the flesh.
- ii. 1 Timothy 4:1-3 - 1 Now the Spirit expressly says that in later times some will depart from the faith by **devoting themselves to deceitful spirits and teachings of demons**, 2 through the insincerity of liars whose consciences are seared, 3 who forbid marriage and **require abstinence from foods that God created to be received with thanksgiving** by those who believe and know the truth.

e. Fasting for spiritual power or for miracles, signs, and wonders is misdirected at heart.
- i. God looks at the motive of fasting.

10. The fast God desires is not about food. It is a heart that is genuinely devoted to Him and will "fast" from selfishness to pour out their lives for others.

a. God desires true humility, worship, and contrition for sin. God desires love for Him and love for our neighbor as for ourself.
- i. Isaiah 58:5-7 - 5 **Is such the fast that I choose, a day for a person to humble himself?** Is it to **bow down his head like a reed**, and to spread sackcloth and ashes under him? Will you call this a fast, and a day acceptable to the LORD? 6 **Is not this the fast that I choose: to loose the bonds of wickedness**, to undo the straps of the yoke, **to let the oppressed go free**, and to break every yoke? 7 Is it not **to share your bread with the hungry and bring the homeless poor into your house; when you see the naked, to cover him, and not to hide yourself from your own flesh?**

b. God desires justice and mercy among His people, not oppression and evil.
- i. Zechariah 7:9-10 - 9 "Thus says the LORD of hosts, **Render true judgments, show kindness and mercy to one another**, 10 **do not oppress** the widow, the fatherless, the sojourner, or the poor, and **let none of you devise evil against another in your heart**."

Unit Six: Humble Yourself Before Man: The Lowest Place

> But when you are invited, go and sit in the lowest place, so that when your host comes he may say to you, 'Friend, move up higher.' Then you will be honored in the presence of all who sit at table with you.
>
> Luke 14:10

A. The Lowest Place

1. Luke 14:7-11 - 7 Now he told a parable to those who were invited, when **he noticed how they chose the places of honor**, saying to them, 8 "When you are invited by someone to a wedding feast, **do not sit down in a place of honor**, lest someone more distinguished than you be invited by him, 9 and he who invited you both will come and say to you, 'Give your place to this person,' and then you will begin with shame to take the lowest place. 10 But **when you are invited, go and sit in the lowest place, so that when your host comes he may say to you, 'Friend, move up higher.' Then you will be honored in the presence of all who sit at table with you**. 11 For everyone who exalts himself will be humbled, and he who humbles himself will be exalted."

   a. Pharisees took the best seats to exalt themselves in the eyes of men. They were posturing for their own advantage and to look important.

   b. Proverbs 25:6-7a - 6 **Do not put yourself forward in the king's presence or stand in the place of the great**, 7 for it is better to be told, "Come up here," than to be put lower in the presence of a noble.

B. Not Seeking Glory from Man

1. Jesus frequently charged people to tell no one what He had done for them. He was not trying to stir up a following for Himself. His entire purpose was to work the mercy of God in people's lives.

   a. Silencing demons who knew who He was.
      i. Luke 4:41 - 41 And demons also came out of many, crying, "You are the Son of God!" But he rebuked them and **would not allow them to speak, because they knew that he was the Christ**.

   b. After healing a leper.
      i. Luke 5:14 - 14 And **he charged him to tell no one**, but "go and show yourself to the priest, and make an offering for your cleansing, as Moses commanded, for a proof to them."

   c. After healing a deaf and mute man.
      i. Mark 7:36 - 36 And **Jesus charged them to tell no one**. But the more he charged them, the more zealously they proclaimed it.

d. After raising a girl from the dead.
   i. Luke 8:56 - 56 And her parents were amazed, but **he charged them to tell no one** what had happened.

e. After the disciples confess that Jesus is the Messiah and Son of God.
   i. Matthew 16:20 - 20 Then **he strictly charged the disciples to tell no one** that he was the Christ.

f. After the transfiguration.
   i. Matthew 17:9 - 9 And as they were coming down the mountain, Jesus commanded them, "**Tell no one the vision, until the Son of Man is raised from the dead**."

2. Jesus went around secretly and often separated Himself from the crowds by retreating into the wilderness.

   a. John 7:2-10 - 2 Now the Jews' Feast of Booths was at hand. 3 So his brothers said to him, "Leave here and go to Judea, **that your disciples also may see the works you are doing**. 4 **For no one works in secret if he seeks to be known openly. If you do these things, show yourself to the world**." 5 For not even his brothers believed in him. 6 Jesus said to them, "My time has not yet come, but your time is always here. 7 The world cannot hate you, but it hates me because I testify about it that its works are evil. 8 You go up to the feast. I am not going up to this feast, for my time has not yet fully come." 9 After saying this, he remained in Galilee. 10 But after his brothers had gone up to the feast, **then he also went up, not publicly but in private**.
      i. His brothers thought that Jesus was making a name for Himself through His ministry, as was the custom of other rabbis in that day. They wanted Him to put Himself on display for His followers and the whole world to see His works.
      ii. Jesus' mission was not to make a name for Himself but to display the righteousness of God which proves and proclaims that the world is evil.
      iii. As a Jewish male under Law, Jesus was required to go to the Feast of Tabernacles. He fulfilled the Law perfectly and went to the Feast. But He did not go with a public entourage to make a display of Himself. He went secretly. He taught at the Temple what the Father told Him to teach.

   b. Mark 1:45 - 45 But he [the cleansed leper whom Jesus had commanded not to tell anyone] went out and began to talk freely about it, and to spread the news, **so that Jesus could no longer openly enter a town, but was out in desolate places**, and people were coming to him from every quarter.
      i. If Jesus were seeking the spotlight, He would have taken advantage of His notoriety and popularity to advance His agenda. Instead, He went to desolate places.

3. Sermon on the Mount: Doing in Secret

   a. Giving in secret.
      i. Matthew 6:1-4 - 1 "**Beware of practicing your righteousness before other people in order to be seen by them,** for then you will have no reward from your Father who is in heaven. 2 "Thus, **when you give to the needy, sound no trumpet before you**, as the hypocrites do in the synagogues and in the streets, that they may be praised by others. Truly, I say to you, they have received their reward. 3 But **when you give to the needy, do not let your left hand know what your right hand is doing**, 4 **so that your giving may be in secret**. And your Father who sees in secret will reward you.

- 01. Not doing it to be seen. No announcements. No name recognition.
- 02. As confidential and secret as possible to receive no credit from anyone except the Lord.

b. Praying in secret.
- i. Matthew 6:5-6 - 5 "**And when you pray, you must not be like the hypocrites. For they love to stand and pray in the synagogues and at the street corners**, that they may be seen by others. Truly, I say to you, they have received their reward. 6 But **when you pray, go into your room and shut the door and pray to your Father who is in secret.** And your Father who sees in secret will reward you.
  - 01. Not public displays or large gatherings on the streets.

c. Fasting without display.
- i. Matthew 6:16-18 - 16 "**And when you fast, do not look gloomy like the hypocrites, for they disfigure their faces** that their fasting may be seen by others. Truly, I say to you, they have received their reward. 17 But **when you fast, anoint your head and wash your face**, 18 **that your fasting may not be seen by others but by your Father who is in secret**. And your Father who sees in secret will reward you.
  - 01. Not displaying weakness or religiosity. Not seeking attention for fasting.

d. A single eye. Seeking earthly reward for our service to God is selfish, self-serving, and evil.
- i. Matthew 6:19-23 KJV - 19 **Lay not up for yourselves treasures upon earth**, where moth and rust doth corrupt, and where thieves break through and steal: 20 **But lay up for yourselves treasures in heaven**, where neither moth nor rust doth corrupt, and where thieves do not break through nor steal: 21 For where your treasure is, there will your heart be also. 22 **The light of the body is the eye: if therefore thine eye be single, thy whole body shall be full of light. 23 But if thine eye be evil, thy whole body shall be full of darkness. If therefore the light that is in thee be darkness, how great is that darkness!**
  - 01. Laying up treasures in heaven is done through acts of selfless giving of ourselves to God and His purposes.
  - 02. If are outwardly "serving the Lord" but our motive is for our own exaltation or benefit, we are deeply deceived.

4. Paul was not seeking glory from man but only from God.

a. Galatians 1:1-10 - 1 Paul, an apostle--**not from men nor through man, but through Jesus Christ and God the Father**, who raised him from the dead-- 2 and all the brothers who are with me, To the churches of Galatia: 3 Grace to you and peace from God our Father and the Lord Jesus Christ, 4 who gave himself for our sins to deliver us from the present evil age, according to the will of our God and Father, 5 to whom be the glory forever and ever. Amen. 6 I am astonished that you are so quickly deserting him who called you in the grace of Christ and are turning to a different gospel-- 7 not that there is another one, but there are some who trouble you and want to distort the gospel of Christ. 8 But even if we or an angel from heaven should preach to you a gospel contrary to the one we preached to you, let him be accursed. 9 As we have said before, so now I say again: If anyone is preaching to you a gospel contrary to the one you received, let him be accursed. 10 **For am I now seeking the approval of man, or of God? Or am I trying to please man? If I were still trying to please man, I would not be a servant of Christ.**
- i. Paul knew that his call to apostleship was from God and not from any man. He was totally uncompromising in his stance of purity in the gospel, to the extent of cursing and denouncing those who do not preach correctly.

ii. He was not seeking to please any man. Man pleasing would make him a servant of man rather than a servant of Christ.

b. 1 Thessalonians 2:3-6 - 3 For **our appeal does not spring from error or impurity or any attempt to deceive**, 4 but just as we have been approved by God to be entrusted with the gospel, so **we speak, not to please man, but to please God who tests our hearts.** 5 **For we never came with words of flattery, as you know, nor with a pretext for greed--God is witness.** 6 **Nor did we seek glory from people, whether from you or from others**, though we could have made demands as apostles of Christ.
    i. Paul's motives in proclaiming the gospel were pure and unselfish.

5. CONTRAST: Instead of puffing up our image to appear strong and mighty, our weaknesses are often what allow God to show Himself mighty through us and/or on our behalf.

    a. 2 Corinthians 13:4 - 4 **For he was crucified in weakness**, but lives by the power of God. For we also are weak in him, but in dealing with you we will live with him by the power of God.

    b. 2 Corinthians 12:9-10 - 9 But he said to me, "My grace is sufficient for you, for **my power is made perfect in weakness.**" Therefore **I will boast all the more gladly of my weaknesses, so that the power of Christ may rest upon me.** 10 For the sake of Christ, then, I am content with weaknesses, insults, hardships, persecutions, and calamities. **For when I am weak, then I am strong**.

    c. 2 Corinthians 1:8-10 - 8 For we do not want you to be unaware, brothers, of the affliction we experienced in Asia. For **we were so utterly burdened beyond our strength that we despaired of life itself**. 9 Indeed, we felt that we had received the sentence of death. **But that was to make us rely not on ourselves but on God who raises the dead**.

6. CONTRAST: Instead of posturing and performing to make ourselves look good in front of one another, we are to openly confess our faults and failures to one another and ask for prayer.

    a. James 5:16 - 16 Therefore, **confess your sins** to one another and pray for one another, that you may be healed. The prayer of a righteous person has great power as it is working.
        i. The King James Version translates this as "confess your faults."

    b. No blame shifting.
        i. Since the Garden of Eden, shifting the blame to another person has been the way of mankind. Adam blamed the woman and the woman blamed the serpent.
        ii. It must not be so among believers whom Jesus died for. Our sins are already forgiven by the blood of Jesus. The blame was already shifted to Him. Therefore, we can openly admit our failings because Jesus has already taken the penalty for them.
        iii. If we will not confess and renounce them, we will not walk in liberty that Christ has for us.

    c. No excuses.
        i. Excuses are given by people who never really wanted to do right. Their excuse places higher priority on something other than obeying God. It is rebellion.
        ii. Explanations are given by people who sincerely tried but were unable to do right.
        iii. An explanation is not an excuse. An explanation does not make wrong right.

C. No Lording Over People

1. The way of the world is to take the highest place possible for your station and use it to your advantage over others. Even religious leaders can function in the way of the world by exalting themselves over others and demanding titles and positions to exert authority over others.

    a. Luke 22:25-27 - 25 And he said to them, "**The kings of the Gentiles exercise lordship over them, and those in authority over them are called benefactors.** 26 **But not so with you.** Rather, let the greatest among you become as the youngest, and the leader as one who serves. 27 For who is the greater, one who reclines at table or one who serves? Is it not the one who reclines at table? **But I am among you as the one who serves**.
        i. Jesus did not demand service but came to serve.

    b. Matthew 23:5-12 - 5 They do all their deeds to be seen by others. For they make their phylacteries broad and their fringes long, 6 and **they love the place of honor at feasts and the best seats in the synagogues** 7 and **greetings in the marketplaces and being called rabbi by others**. 8 But **you are not to be called rabbi**, for you have one teacher, and you are all brothers. 9 And **call no man your father on earth**, for you have one Father, who is in heaven. 10 **Neither be called instructors**, for you have one instructor, the Christ. 11 **The greatest among you shall be your servant.** 12 **Whoever exalts himself will be humbled, and whoever humbles himself will be exalted**.
        i. Jesus did not demand to be called the Messiah or King or refer to Himself as the Messiah. He referred to Himself as the Son of Man – the son of Adam.
        ii. Jesus did not use a title to distinguish Himself over His brothers.
        iii. His example demonstrates how He commands us to be.

2. Kings were commanded to write and meditate on God's Law so that they would not become exalted in their own minds above their brothers.

    a. Deuteronomy 17:18-20 - 18 "And when he sits on the throne of his kingdom, he shall write for himself in a book a copy of this law, approved by the Levitical priests. 19 And it shall be with him, and he shall read in it all the days of his life, **that he may learn to fear the LORD** his God by keeping all the words of this law and these statutes, and doing them, 20 **that his heart may not be lifted up above his brothers**, and **that he may not turn aside from the commandment**, either to the right hand or to the left, so that he may continue long in his kingdom, he and his children, in Israel.

3. Jesus washed His disciples feet as they ultimate example of humble service by the one who is Lord and could have lorded over people.

    a. John 13:3-7, 12-17 - 3 Jesus, **knowing that the Father had given all things into his hands, and that he had come from God and was going back to God**, 4 rose from supper. He laid aside his outer garments, and taking a towel, tied it around his waist. 5 Then he poured water into a basin and **began to wash the disciples' feet** and to wipe them with the towel that was wrapped around him. 6 He came to Simon Peter, who said to him, "Lord, do you wash my feet?" 7 Jesus answered him, "What I am doing you do not understand now, but afterward you will understand." ... 12 When he had washed their feet and put on his outer garments and resumed his place, he said to them, "**Do you understand what I have done to you? 13 You call me Teacher and Lord, and you are right, for so I am. 14 If I then, your Lord and Teacher, have washed your feet, you also ought to wash one another's feet. 15 For I have given you an example, that you also should do just as I have done to you. 16 Truly, truly, I say**

to you, **a servant is not greater than his master, nor is a messenger greater than the one who sent him. 17 If you know these things, blessed are you if you do them**.
- i. God in the flesh, rather than demanding worship or lording over people (which He could have rightfully done) instead came to pour Himself out for the benefit of others.
- ii. Instead of being served as a King, Jesus gave His life for the least of these.

b. Mark 10:45 - 45 **For even the Son of Man came not to be served but to serve**, and to **give his life** as a ransom for many.

D. Submit to One Another & to Authorities

1. Ephesians 5:21 - 21 **submitting to one another out of reverence for Christ**.

   > <u>Submit</u>: Greek-G5293: *hypotasso*: 1. Arrange under, to subordinate. 2. To subject one's self, obey. 3. To submit to one's control. 4. To yield to one's admonition or advice. *This word was a Greek military term meaning "to arrange [troop divisions] in a military fashion under the command of a leader". In non-military use, it was "a voluntary attitude of giving in, cooperating, assuming responsibility, and carrying a burden".*

   a. We are to submit to one another, arranging ourselves under one another, as we arrange ourselves under the direction of Christ.

2. Example of husbands and wives. These passages were written for husbands and wives in a first century Greco-Roman setting but is indicative of the behavior God desires among all of us towards one another.

   a. Cultural Background: In the culture in that day, wives were the property of the husbands. The husband had total authority over the household to dictate all matters. It was the husband's right to run his household like his own Roman empire.

   b. However, in the Church and New Covenant, male and female had been made equal partners in salvation.
   - i. Galatians 3:28 - 28 There is neither Jew nor Greek, there is neither slave nor free, **there is no male and female**, for you are all one in Christ Jesus.
   - ii. Just because wives were equal partners with their husbands in the Gospel, did not authorize rebellion against his authority as the head of the household.
   - iii. A rebellious wife is not a good demonstration of Christ. It fails to reveal the humility and obedience of Jesus.
     - 01. The outside world seeing a rebellious wife will have little respect for the head of the household.
     - 02. The outside world seeing a submissive wife will see kindness and goodness.
   - iv. A domineering husband is a not a good demonstration of Christ. It fails to reveal the sacrificial love and generosity of Jesus.
     - 01. The outside world seeing a domineering or abusive husband will have no desire to participate in his household.
     - 02. The outside world seeing a loving husband will see dignity, self-control, mercy, kindness, humanity, tenderness, etc.

c. Ephesians 5:24-27 - 24 **Now as the church submits to Christ**, so also **wives should submit in everything to their husbands. 25 Husbands, love your wives, as Christ loved the church and gave himself up for her**, 26 that he might sanctify her, having cleansed her by the washing of water with the word, 27 so that he might present the church to himself in splendor, without spot or wrinkle or any such thing, that she might be holy and without blemish.
    i. All of us should be willing to arrange ourselves under one another so that the will of the Lord is done.
    ii. All of us should be willing to lay our lives down for one another as Christ did for us.
    iii. All of us should be aimed at sanctifying one another to present one another to Christ as a mature bride.

d. 1 Peter 3:1-7 - 1 Likewise, **wives, be subject [submit] to your own husbands**, so that even if some do not obey the word, they may be **won without a word by the conduct** of their wives, 2 when they see your **respectful and pure conduct**. 3 Do not let your adorning be external-- the braiding of hair and the putting on of gold jewelry, or the clothing you wear-- 4 but let your adorning be the **hidden person of the heart with the imperishable beauty of a gentle and quiet spirit, which in God's sight is very precious**. 5 For this is how the holy women who hoped in God used to adorn themselves, by submitting to their own husbands, 6 as Sarah obeyed Abraham, calling him lord. And you are her children, if you **do good and do not fear anything that is frightening**. 7 Likewise, **husbands, live with your wives in an understanding way, showing honor to the woman as the weaker vessel**, since they are **heirs with you** of the grace of life, **so that your prayers may not be hindered.**
    i. Submissiveness is an example of Christ's good conduct to win the lost. It is precious in God's sight.
    ii. Submission without fear demonstrates greater faith in God's plan, purpose, and protection of us than in man.
    iii. We must all be conscious of and willing to sacrifice and honor the weaker brother. (See Romans 14.)
    iv. Failure to be submissive or considerate will hinder our own prayers to God. It shows that something is not right in our own hearts. Pride. Arrogance. Superiority.

3. Example of slaves and masters. This is in the first century Greco-Roman setting of slaves and masters but is indicative of the behavior God desires among all of us towards one another.

    a. Cultural Background: In the world in that day, slaves were property of their masters and were sometimes subjected to cruel masters. Indentured servants served for benefits but still had no personal rights to oppose the master of the house.

    b. However, in the church and New Covenant, slaves and masters had been made equal as brothers and sisters.
        i. Galatians 3:28 - 28 There is neither Jew nor Greek, **there is neither slave nor free**, there is no male and female, for you are all one in Christ Jesus.
        ii. 1 Corinthians 12:13 - 13 For in one Spirit we were all baptized into one body--Jews or Greeks, **slaves or free--and all were made to drink of one Spirit.**
        iii. Just because the slaves had been made equals in the Gospel, did not authorize rebellious behavior or attitudes against their masters.
        iv. A rebellious slave is not a good demonstration of Christ. It fails to reveal the submission of Jesus who allowed Himself to be crucified at the hands of sinners.
            01. The outside world seeing a rebellious slave would not see God's decency and order and would have little respect for the God of the household.

- 02. The outside world seeing a submitted slave would be drawn to wonder how to get such good help.
  - v. A domineering master is not a good demonstration of Christ. It fails to reveal the lowliness, servanthood, and shepherding of Jesus, even though He is King.
    - 01. The outside world seeing a harsh master sees someone with a temper.
    - 02. The outside world seeing a considerate master sees dignity, self-control, human decency, etc.

- c. 1 Corinthians 7:21-23 - 21 Were you a bondservant when called? Do not be concerned about it. (But if you can gain your freedom, avail yourself of the opportunity.) 22 For **he who was called in the Lord as a bondservant is a freedman of the Lord**. Likewise **he who was free when called is a bondservant of Christ**. 23 You were bought with a price; do not become bondservants of men.
  - i. Note: Being a slave/servant in this world was not Paul's primary concern. All of those earthly distinctions were nullified through the cross of Christ even though they remain in the natural.
  - ii. All of us have been set free by the death and resurrection of Jesus, no longer subject to the labels of this world for our identify.
  - iii. All of us are to live our lives as slaves of Christ, submitted to Him in every way.

- d. Colossians 3:22-4:1 - 22 **Bondservants, obey in everything those who are your earthly masters, not by way of eye-service, as people-pleasers, but with sincerity of heart, fearing the Lord**. 23 Whatever you do, **work heartily, as for the Lord** and not for men, 24 knowing that from the Lord you will receive the inheritance as your reward. You are serving the Lord Christ. 25 For the wrongdoer will be paid back for the wrong he has done, and there is no partiality. 4:1 **Masters, treat your bondservants justly and fairly**, knowing that you also have a Master in heaven.
  - i. We must all do what we do completely, sincerely, with excellence, and as if we were doing it for the Lord, not to be seen by men.
  - ii. We must all be fair and just in our dealings with one another. We will all be judged.

- e. Ephesians 6:5-9 - 5 **Bondservants, obey your earthly masters with fear and trembling, with a sincere heart, as you would Christ**, 6 not by the way of eye-service, as people-pleasers, but **as bondservants of Christ,** doing the will of God from the heart, 7 **rendering service with a good will as to the Lord and not to man**, 8 knowing that whatever good anyone does, this he will receive back from the Lord, whether he is a bondservant or is free. 9 **Masters, do the same to them, and stop your threatening**, knowing that he who is both their Master and yours is in heaven, and that there is no partiality with him.
  - i. We must all render our service to others with good will towards them, as servants of the Lord, not men.
  - ii. We must all be kind to one another, not threatening violence or punishment, because we will all face judgment from One who is impartial.

4. Submit to church leaders. Even though you are equal before God as brothers and sisters, they have been appointed by God to a position of responsibility in God's House.

   a. Hebrews 13:17 - 17 **Obey your leaders and submit to them**, for they are keeping watch over your souls, as those who will have to give an account. Let them do this with joy and not with groaning, for that would be of no advantage to you.

b. 1 Thessalonians 5:12-13 - 12 We ask you, brothers, **to respect those who labor among you and are over you in the Lord and admonish you**, 13 and to **esteem them very highly in love because of their work**. Be at peace among yourselves.

c. 1 Corinthians 16:15-16 - 15 Now I urge you, brothers--you know that the household of Stephanas were the first converts in Achaia, and that they have devoted themselves to the service of the saints-- 16 **be subject to such as these, and to every fellow worker and laborer.**

5. Submit to the authorities appointed by God. God is not the author of rebellion. Rebellion is arrogance and self-exaltation.

    a. Moses did not lead a rebellion.
        i. According to the command of God, Moses pleaded ten times with Pharaoh to release God's people.

    b. David did not lead a rebellion.
        i. David fled to the wilderness for his life when Saul sought to kill him.
        ii. Even though he had multiple chances to put Saul to death, he refused to lay a hand on the Lord's anointed.
        iii. Even though the Spirit of the Lord had departed from Saul and Saul was in severe rebellion against God, Saul had not been removed him from his position as of King of Israel. David honored that.

    c. Jesus did not lead a rebellion.
        i. Jesus taught the truth and submitted perfectly to the Law of God.
        ii. He did not make any attempts to usurp the authority of the High Priest, Priests, Levites, or Sanhedrin. He demonstrated a higher authority.

6. Submit to the governing authorities in this world. All authority is appointed by God. Therefore, we must honor and submit to them as God's ministers.

    a. Romans 13:1-7 - 1 **Let every person be subject to the governing authorities. For there is no authority except from God, and those that exist have been instituted by God**. 2 Therefore whoever resists the authorities resists what God has appointed, and those who resist will incur judgment. 3 For rulers are not a terror to good conduct, but to bad. Would you have no fear of the one who is in authority? Then do what is good, and you will receive his approval, 4 **for he is God's servant for your good**. But if you do wrong, be afraid, for he does not bear the sword in vain. **For he is the servant of God, an avenger who carries out God's wrath** on the wrongdoer. 5 **Therefore one must be in subjection, not only to avoid God's wrath but also for the sake of conscience**. 6 For because of this you also pay taxes, for the authorities are ministers of God, attending to this very thing. 7 Pay to all what is owed to them: taxes to whom taxes are owed, revenue to whom revenue is owed, respect to whom respect is owed, honor to whom honor is owed.
        i. God's justice is on a bigger picture and timeframe than our short-sighted view.

    b. 1 Peter 2:13-17 - 13 **Be subject for the Lord's sake to every human institution, whether it be to the emperor as supreme, 14 or to governors as sent by him to punish those who do evil and to praise those who do good. 15 For this is the will of God**, that by doing good you should put to silence the ignorance of foolish people. 16 Live as people who are free, not using your freedom as a cover-up for evil, but living as servants of God. 17 Honor everyone. Love the brotherhood. Fear God. **Honor the emperor.**

7. Jesus submit Himself to the governing authorities because He knew they were appointed by God to do God's work.

    a. John 19:10-11 - 10 So Pilate said to him, "You will not speak to me? **Do you not know that I have authority to release you and authority to crucify you?**" 11 Jesus answered him, "**You would have no authority over me at all unless it had been given you from above**. Therefore he who delivered me over to you has the greater sin."
        i. Jesus did not argue His case or defend Himself before Pilate or Herod, the ones whom God had appointed as authorities in His territories in that day.
        ii. He did not resist arrest. He did not call for the supernatural help of angels.
        iii. He allowed Himself to be led like a lamb to slaughter.

8. Pray FOR those in authority. Unless they come to know Jesus, leaders of this world are already condemned to Babylon's doom will be judged for their immorality with the harlot's system.

    a. 1 Timothy 2:1-4 - 1 First of all, then, **I urge that supplications, prayers, intercessions, and thanksgivings be made for all people**, 2 **for kings and all who are in high positions**, that we may lead a peaceful and quiet life, godly and dignified in every way. 3 This is good, and it is pleasing in the sight of God our Savior, 4 who desires all people to be saved and to come to the knowledge of the truth.

E. Honor God in Others

1. Spiritual gifts in the Body of Christ. Other people have gifts from God that you need to receive from them.

    a. Romans 12:3-6a - 3 For by the grace given to me I say to everyone among you **not to think of himself more highly than he ought to think**, but to think with sober judgment, each according to the measure of faith that God has assigned. 4 For **as in one body we have many members, and the members do not all have the same function**, 5 **so we, though many, are one body in Christ, and individually members one of another**. 6 Having **gifts that differ according to the grace given to us**, let us use them:

    b. 1 Corinthians 12:12-21 - 12 **For just as the body is one and has many members, and all the members of the body, though many, are one body, so it is with Christ**. 13 For in one Spirit we were all baptized into one body--Jews or Greeks, slaves or free--and all were made to drink of one Spirit. 14 **For the body does not consist of one member but of many**. 15 If the foot should say, "Because I am not a hand, I do not belong to the body," that would not make it any less a part of the body. 16 And if the ear should say, "Because I am not an eye, I do not belong to the body," that would not make it any less a part of the body. 17 If the whole body were an eye, where would be the sense of hearing? If the whole body were an ear, where would be the sense of smell? 18 **But as it is, God arranged the members in the body, each one of them, as he chose**. 19 If all were a single member, where would the body be? 20 **As it is, there are many parts, yet one body**. 21 The eye cannot say to the hand, "I have no need of you," nor again the head to the feet, "I have no need of you."

2. Honor God speaking to you through other believers and through His prophets.

    a. Remember that all sons and daughters of God can prophesy. (Acts 2:17-18.)

b. There are many Old Testament examples of people who refused to humble themselves to listen to God's counsel through His prophets. This is a mistake.
   i. 2 Chronicles 36:15-16 - 15 The LORD, the God of their fathers, **sent persistently to them by his messengers, because he had compassion on his people** and on his dwelling place. 16 **But they kept mocking the messengers of God, despising his words and scoffing at his prophets**, until the wrath of the LORD rose against his people, until there was no remedy.

c. 2 Chronicles 20:20b – 20b Believe in the LORD your God, and you will be established; **believe his prophets, and you will succeed**.

d. 1 Thessalonians 5:19-21 - 19 Do not quench the Spirit. 20 **Do not despise prophecies,** 21 **but test everything**; hold fast what is good.

e. Matthew 10:40-41 - 40 "**Whoever receives you receives me**, and whoever receives me receives him who sent me. 41 **The one who receives a prophet because he is a prophet will receive a prophet's reward**, and the one who receives a righteous person because he is a righteous person will receive a righteous person's reward.

f. Remember: prophecies are subject to interpretation. Paul received numerous prophecies that if he went to Jerusalem, he would be tortured. Therefore, people urged him not to go. However, Paul knew that he must go and was willing to give his life for the Lord.
   i. Acts 21:10-14 - 10 While we were staying for many days, a prophet named Agabus came down from Judea. 11 And coming to us, he took Paul's belt and bound his own feet and hands and said, 'Thus says the Holy Spirit, 'This is how the Jews at Jerusalem will bind the man who owns this belt and deliver him into the hands of the Gentiles.'" 12 When we heard this, **we and the people there urged him not to go up to Jerusalem**. 13 **Then Paul answered, "What are you doing, weeping and breaking my heart? For I am ready not only to be imprisoned but even to die in Jerusalem for the name of the Lord Jesus**." 14 And since he would not be persuaded, we ceased and said, "Let the will of the Lord be done."

3. Honor that God created and is sovereign over unbelievers, particularly those in authority. Do not be haughty against authorities just because they are unbelievers.

   a. Proverbs 16:10 - 10 **An oracle is on the lips of a king; his mouth does not sin in judgment**.
      i. The king is speaking the Lord's will whether it looks righteous or not. God uses authorities in the earth to enact his justice upon faithful or rebellious people. Even poor judgments from the king are part of how God implements justice. Consider Pharaoh and his hardened heart.
      ii. Example: Rehoboam's harshness with the people of Israel was the will of God to cause the division of the Kingdom due to Solomon's sins. It was the fulfillment of what God had decreed and ordained for His people. (1 Kings 12; 2 Chronicles 10.)

   b. God gives wisdom to Kings for His purposes whether they acknowledge Him or not.
      i. Example: Pharaoh's dreams about the impending famine. (Genesis 41.)
      ii. Example: Pharaoh knowing Sarah was Abraham's wife when plagues broke out. (Genesis 12.)
      iii. Example: Abimelech's dream that God was punishing him for taking Sarah as his wife. (Genesis 20.)

iv. Example: Nebuchadnezzar guided by God through divination to attack Jerusalem. (Ezekiel 21.)
v. Example: Nebuchadnezzar's dream of the world empires to come. (Daniel 2.)
vi. Example: Cyrus decreed the return of the Jews to their land, even though he did not know God. (Isaiah 45; 2 Chronicles 36; Ezra 1.)
vii. Example: The wise men did not to return to Herod after meeting Jesus because of a dream. (Matthew 2.)
viii. Example: Even though Caiaphas rejected Jesus, he prophesied accurately about Jesus' death for the people because he was the High Priest. (John 11:51.)

c. Haughtiness or presumption against unbelievers in authority will not go well.
i. Example: Abraham lied two times because he thought to himself, "There is no fear of God in this place." (Genesis 13 and 20.)
01. Isaac did the same thing with Rebekah. (Genesis 26.)
ii. Example: Josiah died in battle because he did not believe that God had directed Pharaoh, even though Pharaoh openly said so. (2 Chronicles 35:20-24.)

F. Not to Condemn but to Save

1. Don't judge. Remove the plank from your own eye so that you can help your brother.

    a. Matthew 7:1-5 - 1 **Judge not, that you be not judged**. 2 For with the judgment you pronounce you will be judged, and with the measure you use it will be measured to you. 3 **Why do you see the speck that is in your brother's eye, but do not notice the log that is in your own eye?** 4 Or how can you say to your brother, 'Let me take the speck out of your eye,' when there is the log in your own eye? 5 **You hypocrite, first take the log out of your own eye, and then you will see clearly to take the speck out of your brother's eye**.

    b. This does not mean do not judge anything or anyone. It means you are a hypocrite if you have not first repented of the same sin in your own life.
    i. Note: Typically, those who are offended by someone else's behavior are guilty of the very same behavior themselves even if it does not manifest exactly the same way.
    ii. Note: If the person never struggled in that area, it is easy to have mercy. If, with the Lord's help. a person has conquered that area, they will have useful sympathy and compassion. It is only those who are still guilty of the same offense that are easily offended and stand in judgment of those doing the very things they are guilty of.

2. Ministry of Reconciliation

    a. 2 Corinthians 5:18-19 - 18 All this is from God, who through Christ reconciled us to himself and gave us the **ministry of reconciliation**; 19 that is, in Christ God was reconciling the world to himself, **not counting their trespasses against them**, and entrusting to us the **message of reconciliation**.

    b. It's GOOD NEWS – the world is already condemned to hell. But God has made a way for them to be saved.
    i. Condemning others is equivalent to exalting ourselves above them, as if we were not also in need of Jesus as our Savior.

3. The Law of Liberty

   a. James 1:25; 2:8-13 - 25 But the **one who looks into the perfect law, the law of liberty**, and perseveres, being no hearer who forgets but a doer who acts, he will be blessed in his doing. ... 2:8 If you really fulfill **the royal law according to the Scripture**, "You shall love your neighbor as yourself," you are doing well. 9 But if you show partiality, you are committing sin and are **convicted by the law as transgressors**. 10 For whoever keeps the whole law but fails in one point has become guilty of all of it. 11 For he who said, "Do not commit adultery," also said, "Do not murder." If you do not commit adultery but do murder, you have become a transgressor of the law. 12 **So speak and so act as those who are to be judged under the law of liberty**. 13 **For judgment is without mercy to one who has shown no mercy. Mercy triumphs over judgment**.

   b. The perfect law or law of liberty is the law of Christ who liberated us from the law of sin and death. The perfect law is God's heart of MERCY.

   c. The royal law is the Law of Moses, summarized as "Love your neighbor as yourself" and the listing of the ten commandments. We are no longer under this Law.
      i. One transgression against the royal law disqualifies a person from all of its blessings.
      ii. Christ died to liberate us from this Law. No one has ever fulfilled it, except Jesus.

   d. We are called to the standard of the law of liberty – to show MERCY by not holding offenses against people. Mercy triumphs over judgment. We are called to show mercy.

   e. If we fail to show mercy to others, we demonstrate that we have failed to understand Christ's forgiveness for us and that He liberated us from sin and the rightful demands of repayment. Therefore, there will be no mercy for us on the day of judgment.

G. Mercy for the Poor – the Fast God Desires

1. Our attitude toward the poor reflects our attitude toward the Lord. If our heart is hard to the poor or we begrudge them, accuse them, or have no mercy for them, we have failed to recognize our own poverty before God and what He has done for us.

   a. Test your attitude toward the poor against the way Jesus died for you.
      i. Example: "They choose to be that way." What if Jesus had said that about you and decided not to save you?
      ii. Example: "They need to get a job." What if Jesus had made you earn your salvation?
      iii. Example: "They're going to use it for the wrong things." What if Jesus did not save you because He knew that you would not always do His will, even after being saved?

2. As you did it to the least of these, you did it to Me.

   a. Matthew 25:34-46 - 34 Then the King will say to those on his right, 'Come, you who are blessed by my Father, inherit the kingdom prepared for you from the foundation of the world. 35 **For I was hungry and you gave me food, I was thirsty and you gave me drink, I was a stranger and you welcomed me,** 36 **I was naked and you clothed me, I was sick and you visited me, I was in prison and you came to me.**' 37 Then the righteous will answer him, saying, 'Lord, when did we see you hungry and feed you, or thirsty and give you drink? 38 And when did we see you a stranger and welcome you, or naked and clothe you? 39 And when did we see you sick or in prison and visit you?' 40 And the King will answer them, 'Truly, I say to you, **as you did it to one of the least of these my brothers, you did it to me.'** 41 "Then he will say to those on his left, 'Depart from me, you cursed, into the eternal fire prepared for the devil and his angels. 42 **For I was hungry and you gave me no food, I was thirsty and you gave me no drink,** 43 **I was a stranger and you did not welcome me, naked and you did not clothe me, sick and in prison and you did not visit me.'** 44 Then they also will answer, saying, 'Lord, when did we see you hungry or thirsty or a stranger or naked or sick or in prison, and did not minister to you?' 45 Then he will answer them, saying, **'Truly, I say to you, as you did not do it to one of the least of these, you did not do it to me.'** 46 And these will go away into eternal punishment, but the righteous into eternal life."

3. The fast God desires.

   a. Isaiah 58:6-10 - 6 "Is not this the fast that I choose: to **loose the bonds of wickedness, to undo the straps of the yoke, to let the oppressed go free, and to break every yoke**? 7 Is it not to **share your bread with the hungry and bring the homeless poor into your house; when you see the naked, to cover him, and not to hide yourself from your own flesh?** 8 Then shall your light break forth like the dawn, and your healing shall spring up speedily; your righteousness shall go before you; the glory of the LORD shall be your rear guard. 9 Then you shall call, and the LORD will answer; you shall cry, and he will say, 'Here I am.' **If you take away the yoke from your midst, the pointing of the finger, and speaking wickedness,** 10 **if you pour yourself out for the hungry and satisfy the desire of the afflicted**, then shall your light rise in the darkness and your gloom be as the noonday.
      i. God does not enjoy religious observance or ascetic fasting.
      ii. True fasting is the giving of ourselves over to the will and purposes of God. To reveal His heart to the hurting and broken rather than judging or hiding ourselves and looking away from other human beings who are just like us.

   b. Zechariah 7:8-10 - 8 And the word of the LORD came to Zechariah, saying, 9 "Thus says the LORD of hosts, **Render true judgments, show kindness and mercy to one another**, 10 **do not oppress the widow, the fatherless, the sojourner, or the poor, and let none of you devise evil against another in your heart."**
      i. True fasting is to abstain from lording over one another, perverting justice for selfish gain, and taking advantage of the vulnerable. True fasting is to fast from evil.

4. Invite those who can never repay you.

   a. Luke 14:12-14 - 12 He said also to the man who had invited him, "When you give a dinner or a banquet, do not invite your friends or your brothers or your relatives or rich neighbors, lest they also invite you in return and you be repaid. 13 But **when you give a feast, invite the poor, the crippled, the lame, the blind,** 14 **and you will be blessed, because they cannot repay you. For you will be repaid at the resurrection of the just."**

   b. Inviting those who can repay us is self-serving for purposes of this world. It is networking for ourselves and our own advantage.

   c. Inviting those who cannot repay us is selfless, God-focused, and will be rewarded in eternity. It is making friends for ourselves in heaven and friends for God.

Unit Seven: Humble Yourself in Trials & Suffering

> Since therefore Christ suffered in the flesh, arm yourselves with the same way of thinking, for whoever has suffered in the flesh has ceased from sin,
>
> 1 Peter 4:1

A. Satan has Asked to Sift You

1. Luke 22:31-34 - 31 "Simon, Simon, behold, **Satan demanded to have you, that he might sift you like wheat,** 32 **but I have prayed for you that your faith may not fail.** And **when you have turned again, strengthen your brothers**." 33 Peter said to him, "Lord, I am ready to go with you both to prison and to death." 34 Jesus said, "I tell you, Peter, the rooster will not crow this day, **until you deny three times that you know me**."

    a. The adversary desires to test the sincerity of our faith.
        i. Sifting wheat is the process of separating the wheat and chaff.
        ii. Chaff is the hard outer coating that protects the tender grain of wheat.
        iii. Wheat is useful for food, chaff is useful for nothing.

        > Deny: Greek-G533: *aparneomai*: 1. To deny. 2. To affirm that one has no acquaintance or connection with someone. 3. To forget one's self and one's own interests. 4. To abstain. 5. To disown.

    b. Mark 14:27-31 - 27 And Jesus said to them, "**You will all fall away, for it is written, 'I will strike the shepherd, and the sheep will be scattered.**' 28 But after I am raised up, I will go before you to Galilee." 29 Peter said to him, "**Even though they all fall away, I will not**." 30 And Jesus said to him, "Truly, I tell you, this very night, before the rooster crows twice, **you will deny me three times**." 31 But he said emphatically, "**If I must die with you, I will not deny you." And they all said the same**.
        i. Jesus knew that all of the disciples would be sifted and prove to be chaff that would fall away in his hour of greatest need.
        ii. Peter was arrogant and lacked self-awareness. Peter proclaimed Jesus as Lord and Messiah with his mouth, but did not know that he still had it in his heart to deny Jesus.
        iii. The disciples all said the same about themselves as Peter exclaimed.

    c. Note: The you in Luke 22, verse 31 is plural, meaning Satan asked to sift all of the disciples. All of the "you" in verse 32 are singular, addressed to Peter. (More on this in point 3)
        i. It could read: Satan demanded to have **you [all]**, that he might sift you like wheat, 32 but I have prayed for **you [Peter]** that your faith may not fail...

2. When the pressure was on, ALL the disciples caved to it and denied Jesus. They lost sight of their eternal best interest for their temporal safety and protection.
    a. Peter denied three times that he knew Jesus. Then, he was crushed to see himself as he really was and what he was capable of doing.

- i. Luke 22:56-62 - 56 Then a servant girl, seeing him as he sat in the light and looking closely at him, said, "This man also was with him." 57 **But he denied it, saying, "Woman, I do not know him**." 58 And a little later someone else saw him and said, "You also are one of them." But **Peter said, "Man, I am not**." 59 And after an interval of about an hour still another insisted, saying, "Certainly this man also was with him, for he too is a Galilean." 60 **But Peter said, "Man, I do not know what you are talking about**." And immediately, while he was still speaking, the rooster crowed. 61 And the Lord turned and looked at Peter. And Peter remembered the saying of the Lord, how he had said to him, "Before the rooster crows today, you will deny me three times." 62 **And he went out and wept bitterly**.

- b. Mark 14:50 - 50 **And they all left him and fled**.
    - i. ALL of the disciples failed and fled in the hour of trial.
    - ii. Note: this was BEFORE the outpouring of the Holy Spirit. After the Holy Spirit was poured out, each of these men went on to give their lives for the Lord, proclaiming the Gospel.

- c. The pressure of trials reveals what we are really made of.
    - i. If we are functioning in the flesh, we will cave to pressure just as they did.
    - ii. If we live by the Spirit, we will stand in the ways of the Lord and not deny Him.

3. Jesus is interceding for our victory.

    a. Jesus prayed for Peter's faith and commanded him to strengthen his brothers after learning the lesson of the siftings of Satan.
    - i. As can be seen in Peter's proclamations in the Book of Acts, Peter did so. His letters strengthened believers against persecution in the world (1 Peter) and false teachers infiltrating the church (2 Peter.)

    b. Jesus lives to intercede for us at the throne of God. (Hebrews 7:25.)
    - i. He is praying for our faith to stand in Him as we face various trials and so that we can then turn and strengthen others in the ways of the Lord.

4. When you turn, strengthen your brothers. Peter became a great encourager of believers who were undergoing trials because he understood God's purpose in it.

    a. 1 Peter 1:6-7 - 6 In this you rejoice, though now for a little while, if necessary, you have been **grieved by various trials, 7 so that the tested genuineness of your faith--more precious than gold that perishes though it is tested by fire**--may be found to result in praise and glory and honor at the revelation of Jesus Christ.

    b. When Jesus returns, believers who have stood their ground to withstand the tests and trials of faith will be proved right in having done so, even though for a little while we may look foolish and defeated in this world.

5. Repentance vs. Remorse

    a. Peter repented. As soon as Peter realized what he had done, he wept bitterly, knowing that he had denied the Lord whom he loved and believed in.

    b. In contrast, Judas had remorse but did not repent. He tried to take matters into his own hands to undo what he had done in betraying Jesus.

i. Matthew 27:3-5 NKJV - 3 Then Judas, His betrayer, seeing that He had been condemned, **was remorseful and brought back the thirty pieces of silver** to the chief priests and elders, 4 saying, "**I have sinned by betraying innocent blood.**" And they said, "What is that to us? You see to it!" 5 Then he threw down the pieces of silver in the temple and departed, and **went and hanged himself.**

6. The fruit of genuine repentance.

    a. 2 Corinthians 7:10-11 - 10 For **godly grief produces a repentance that leads to salvation** without regret, whereas **worldly grief produces death.** 11 For see what **earnestness** this godly grief has produced in you, but also what **eagerness to clear yourselves**, what **indignation**, what **fear**, what **longing**, what **zeal**, what **punishment**! At every point you have proved yourselves innocent in the matter.
        i. Remorse/worldly grief leads only to more death.
        ii. Godly grief is genuine repentance, a true change of the mind, heart, and approach.

    b. As per 2 Corinthians 7:11, The fruit of genuine repentance includes:
        i. <u>Earnestness</u>: Diligence to do differently. Hasty application of new understanding.
        ii. <u>Eagerness to clear (Vindication)</u>: *apologia*, as in apologize. A reasoned statement or argument. Admittance of wrongdoing or profession of innocence.
        iii. <u>Indignation</u>: Vexation, anger or annoyance at having done wrong.
        iv. <u>Fear (of the Lord)</u>: Reverence for the Lord and His ways coupled with willingness to submit to Him.
        v. <u>Longing</u>: Vehement desire to make it right.
        vi. <u>Zeal</u>: Excitement, passion, fervor in pursuing rectification.
        vii. <u>Punishment (Vengeance)</u>: Giving justice to wronged parties by exacting consequence on wrongdoers.

B. Mindset and Perspective in Suffering

1. Jesus prepared His disciples to anticipate persecution and suffering for following Him.

    a. Note: Anticipate but do not expect suffering.
        i. We must walk in faith and hope, not dread, worry, and expectation of trouble.
        ii. When trials come and suffering happens, do not be surprised by it.

    b. John 15:18-21 - 18 "**If the world hates you, know that it has hated me before it hated you.** 19 If you were of the world, the world would love you as its own; but because you are not of the world, but I chose you out of the world, therefore the world hates you. 20 Remember the word that I said to you: **'A servant is not greater than his master.' If they persecuted me, they will also persecute you.** If they kept my word, they will also keep yours. 21 But all these things they will do to you on account of my name, because they do not know him who sent me.

    c. Acts 14:21-22 - 21 When they had preached the gospel to that city and had made many disciples, they returned to Lystra and to Iconium and to Antioch, 22 strengthening the souls of the disciples, encouraging them to continue in the faith, and saying that **through many tribulations we must enter the kingdom of God.**
    d. 2 Timothy 3:12 - 12 Indeed, **all who desire to live a godly life in Christ Jesus will be persecuted.**

- e. 1 Peter 4:1-2 - 1 Since therefore Christ suffered in the flesh, **arm yourselves with the same way of thinking, for whoever has suffered in the flesh has ceased from sin,** 2 so as to live for the rest of the time in the flesh no longer for human passions but for the will of God.
    - i. Peter exhorts us to be prepared to suffer in the flesh – meaning being impacted by physical, bodily harm (i.e. beating, imprisonment, torture, death, etc.)

2. Suffering for righteousness, not for doing wrong.

    - a. 1 Peter 2:18-21 - 18 Servants, be subject to your masters with all respect, not only to the good and gentle but also to the unjust. 19 For **this is a gracious thing, when, mindful of God, one endures sorrows while suffering unjustly.** 20 For **what credit is it if, when you sin and are beaten for it, you endure? But if when you do good and suffer for it you endure, this is a gracious thing in the sight of God.** 21 For **to this you have been called, because Christ also suffered for you, leaving you an example,** so that you might follow in his steps.

    - b. 1 Peter 4:15 - 15 But let none of you suffer as a **murderer or a thief or an evildoer or as a meddler.**
        - i. It is no credit to us in God's sight if we do wrong and receive the just consequence for our error.

    - c. It is only suffering for righteousness' sake if we are following Jesus, obeying His voice, carrying out His commands, and suffer persecution for it.

3. Rejoice in Suffering.

    - a. 1 Peter 4:12-14 - 12 Beloved, **do not be surprised at the fiery trial when it comes upon you to test you,** as though something strange were happening to you. 13 But **rejoice insofar as you share Christ's sufferings,** that you may also rejoice and be glad when his glory is revealed. 14 **If you are insulted for the name of Christ, you are blessed, because the Spirit of glory and of God rests upon you.**
        - i. We should not be surprised by trials. Instead, we should rejoice that we have been counted worthy to suffer for Jesus.
        - ii. When we suffer for Jesus, the glory of God rests upon us.

    - b. Acts 5:40-41 - 40 and when they had called in the apostles, they beat them and charged them not to speak in the name of Jesus, and let them go. 41 Then they left the presence of the council, **rejoicing that they were counted worthy to suffer dishonor for the name.**

    - c. James 1:2-4 - 2 **Count it all joy, my brothers, when you meet trials of various kinds,** 3 for you know that **the testing of your faith produces steadfastness.** 4 And **let steadfastness have its full effect, that you may be perfect and complete, lacking in nothing.**
        - i. We can and should rejoice in trials because they are being used by God to train us in righteousness and conform us totally to the image of Christ.
        - ii. If we encounter and respond to trials correctly, they will work spiritual maturity in us.

    - d. Romans 5:3-5 - 3 Not only that, but **we rejoice in our sufferings, knowing that suffering produces endurance,** 4 **and endurance produces character, and character produces hope,** 5 **and hope does not put us to shame,** because God's love has been poured into our hearts through the Holy Spirit who has been given to us.
        - i. We rejoice in suffering because it grows us in endurance and relying on the power of God rather than our own strength.

ii. We rejoice in suffering because it forces us to set our sights on eternity and not on the things of this world.

4. Learning obedience & becoming a compassionate High Priest.

   a. Hebrews 5:7-8 - 7 In the days of his flesh, Jesus offered up prayers and supplications, with loud cries and tears, to him who was able to save him from death, and he was heard because of his reverence. 8 **Although he was a son, he learned obedience through what he suffered**.
      i. Even Jesus learned obedience through suffering. Jesus endured and fulfilled God's purpose to receive His reward.
      ii. Jesus knows the temptation, especially when under the pressure of severe trials to cave in or deny God in order to avoid suffering.

   b. Hebrews 4:15 - 15 For **we do not have a high priest who is unable to sympathize** with our weaknesses, **but one who in every respect has been tempted as we are, yet without sin**.
      i. Jesus was tested in all points, but without sin. He is our example of a suffering servant who held fast to God in every respect and received His due reward.
      ii. Because Jesus was tested, He is compassionate towards us as we suffer trials and encourages us from His own experience of temptation and suffering.

   c. Like Jesus, when we are willing to undergo God ordained suffering, it demonstrably proves that we are not serving ourselves or our own ambitions but are living for God and His will.
      i. John 8:28 - 28 So Jesus said to them, "**When you have lifted up the Son of Man**, then you will know that I am he, and that **I do nothing on my own authority**, but speak just as the Father taught me."
         01. Allowing Himself to be crucified proved that Jesus was not trying to make a name for Himself but for God.
         02. Anyone functioning under their own authority would take every possible self-protective measure and never allow themselves to suffer.
      ii. John 7:17-18 - 17 If anyone's will is to do God's will, he will know whether the teaching is from God or **whether I am speaking on my own authority**. 18 The one who speaks on his own authority seeks his own glory; but **the one who seeks the glory of him who sent him is true**, and in him there is no falsehood.
         01. Jesus sought the glory of God, even at the expense of His own life. This proved that He was not functioning for His own exaltation, but God's.

   d. Like Jesus, as we endure through suffering, we become more compassionate towards those who are suffering and become better able to help them and comfort them.
      i. 2 Corinthians 1:3-6 - 3 Blessed be the God and Father of our Lord Jesus Christ, the Father of mercies and God of all comfort, 4 **who comforts us in all our affliction, so that we may be able to comfort those who are in any affliction, with the comfort with which we ourselves are comforted by God**. 5 For as we **share abundantly in Christ's sufferings, so through Christ we share abundantly in comfort too**. 6 If we are afflicted, it is for your comfort and salvation; and if we are comforted, it is for your comfort, which you experience when you patiently endure the same sufferings that we suffer.
         01. This is not physical, fleshly, or material comfort.
         02. This is the eternal comfort of the Lord's sovereignty over our lives and our hope of salvation and the world to come.

   e. Like Jesus, as we endure through suffering, we learn obedience to the Lord and grow in our faith in His faithfulness towards us.

i. 2 Timothy 2:11-13 - 11 The saying is trustworthy, for: **If we have died with him, we will also live with him;** 12 **if we endure, we will also reign** with him; **if we deny him, he also will deny us;** 13 **if we are faithless, he remains faithful-- for he cannot deny himself.**

C. Chastisement of God: Treated as Sons

1. Hebrews 12:1-4 - 1 Therefore, since we are surrounded by so great a cloud of witnesses, let us also lay aside every weight, and sin which clings so closely, and let us run with endurance the race that is set before us, 2 **looking to Jesus, the founder and perfecter of our faith, who for the joy that was set before him endured the cross, despising the shame**, and is seated at the right hand of the throne of God. 3 Consider him who **endured from sinners such hostility against himself**, so that you may not grow weary or fainthearted. 4 In your struggle against sin you have not yet resisted to the point of shedding your blood.

    a. The cloud of witnesses from Hebrews 11 testify to God's faithfulness and worthiness. Jesus is the most faithful witness of all and is now seated at the right hand of God.
        i. They are God's glorifiers - extolling and proving the worthiness and truthfulness of God so that we are encouraged to be faithful.
        ii. They are not our personal cheerleaders for our own ambitions and pursuits. In the metaphor of crowd spectating a race, they are watching us pertaining to remaining faithful to God.

    b. Lay aside every weight and sin that entangles, besets, skillfully surrounds us.
        i. We must learn to do things God's way rather than follow our own passions by laying aside and rejecting everything that tries to steer us away from God and obedience to Him.

    c. We follow a sinless, perfect, crucified King – He set the pattern and example of the life of sons of God.
        i. The pattern is death to the flesh and death to this world out of placing utmost importance on eternal life with God.
        ii. The pattern is death to this life to have real life with God forever.

    d. We must keep in mind the suffering of Jesus which far surpasses our sufferings so that we do not grow weary in faith.

2. Hebrews 12:5-11 - 5 And have you forgotten the exhortation that addresses you as sons? "**My son, do not regard lightly the discipline of the Lord, nor be weary when reproved by him.** 6 For **the Lord disciplines the one he loves, and chastises every son whom he receives.**" 7 It is for discipline that you have to endure. **God is treating you as sons**. For what son is there whom his father does not discipline? 8 **If you are left without discipline, in which all have participated, then you are illegitimate children and not sons**. 9 Besides this, we have had earthly fathers who disciplined us and we respected them. Shall we not much more be subject to the Father of spirits and live? 10 For they disciplined us for a short time as it seemed best to them, but **he disciplines us for our good, that we may share his holiness.** 11 **For the moment all discipline seems painful rather than pleasant, but later it yields the peaceful fruit of righteousness to those who have been trained by it.**

> Discipline: Greek-G3811: *paideuo*: 1. To train children. To instruct or cause to learn. 2. To chasten or teach. To correct. Of those who are molding the character of others by reproof and admonition. 3. Of God: to chasten by the affliction of evils and calamities. 4. To chastise with blows. Of a father punishing his son. Of a judge ordering one to be scourged.
>
> Discipline: Greek-3809: *paideia*: 1. Chastening, nurturing, instruction. 2. The whole training and education of children (which relates to the cultivation of the mind and morals, through commands and admonitions, reproofs and punishments.) It includes the training of the body. 3. Whatever in adults also cultivates the soul, especially by correcting mistakes and curbing passions. 4. Instruction which aims at increasing virtue.

- a. Trials in our life are what God uses to teach and train us in His ways, like a loving father helping a son learn the right way to do things.
    - i. Proverbs 3:11-12 - 11 My son, **do not despise the LORD's discipline** or be weary of his reproof, 12 for the LORD reproves him whom he loves, **as a father the son in whom he delights**.
    - ii. Revelation 3:19 - 19 **Those whom I love, I reprove and discipline**, **so be zealous and repent**.

- b. It does not mean that God is working evil against us but in the midst of the evil being worked against us (or that we get ourselves into) God uses the trial to teach us how to respond with righteousness and holiness.
    - i. Most often, it is our own flesh that desires what is in contrast to God's will for us. God will teach us to crucify our flesh so that we live for Him alone.

- c. If we are undisciplined by God, we are illegitimate children and have not been transformed from flesh into His likeness.
    - i. Discipline is painful but effective. Its purpose is to purify a people as the Bride of Christ.

3. Hebrews 12:12-17 - 12 Therefore lift your drooping hands and strengthen your weak knees, 13 and **make straight paths for your feet**, so that what is lame may not be put out of joint but rather be healed. 14 Strive for peace with everyone, and for the holiness without which no one will see the Lord. 15 **See to it that no one fails to obtain the grace of God; that no "root of bitterness" springs up and causes trouble**, and by it many become defiled; 16 **that no one is sexually immoral** or **unholy like Esau, who sold his birthright for a single meal**. 17 For you know that afterward, when he desired to inherit the blessing, he was rejected, for he found no chance to repent, though he sought it with tears.

    a. Be strong and get on the straight, narrow, and difficult path that leads to life.

    b. A root of bitterness occurs when someone among the people of God determines to go their own way and convinces themselves that this is ok in the sight of God.
       - i. Deuteronomy 29:18-19 - 18 Beware lest there be among you a man or woman or clan or tribe **whose heart is turning away today from the LORD** our God to go and serve the gods of those nations. Beware **lest there be among you a root bearing poisonous and bitter fruit, 19 one who, when he hears the words of this sworn covenant, blesses himself in his heart, saying, 'I shall be safe, though I walk in the stubbornness of my heart.'** This will lead to the sweeping away of moist and dry alike.

c. Esau caved to the hungers of his flesh and sold his birthright for carnal satisfaction. We must be careful not to diminish the value of eternal life and what Jesus has done for us.

D. Wilderness 1: Disciplined as Sons

1. Deuteronomy 8:1-6 - 1 "The whole commandment that I command you today you shall be careful to do, that you may live and multiply, and go in and possess the land that the LORD swore to give to your fathers. 2 And you shall remember the whole way that the LORD your God has led you **these forty years in the wilderness, that he might humble you, testing you to know what was in your heart, whether you would keep his commandments or not**. 3 And he **humbled you and let you hunger and fed you with manna**, which you did not know, nor did your fathers know, **that he might make you know that man does not live by bread alone, but man lives by every word that comes from the mouth of the LORD**. 4 Your clothing did not wear out on you and your foot did not swell these forty years. 5 **Know then in your heart that, as a man disciplines his son, the LORD your God disciplines you**. 6 So you shall **keep the commandments** of the LORD your God by walking in his ways and by fearing him.

   a. An entire generation had to die because they did not believe that God was able to give them the Promised Land – even after they had seen God walk them through the parted waters of the Red Sea and bury Pharaoh and the army of Egypt in the depths.
      i. An eleven-day journey took forty years because God would not permit them to enter until that generation passed away.

   b. God's purpose in the wilderness was to humble the people and to test their hearts. Being in a desert wasteland revealed their rebellion and unbelief and trained them to cry out to God and obey His ways.

   c. As a faithful Father, God supplied miraculous bread every day for His people for forty years. The wilderness proved that obeying the commands of God is more important than bread.

2. Deuteronomy 8:11-18 - 11 "Take care lest you forget the LORD your God by not keeping his commandments and his rules and his statutes, which I command you today, 12 **lest, when you have eaten and are full and have built good houses and live in them**, 13 and when your herds and flocks multiply and your silver and gold is multiplied and all that you have is multiplied, 14 then your heart be lifted up, and **you forget the LORD your God, who brought you out of the land of Egypt, out of the house of slavery**, 15 **who led you through the great and terrifying wilderness, with its fiery serpents and scorpions and thirsty ground where there was no water, who brought you water out of the flinty rock**, 16 who fed you in the wilderness with manna that your fathers did not know, **that he might humble you and test you, to do you good in the end**. 17 **Beware lest you say in your heart, 'My power and the might of my hand have gotten me this wealth.'** 18 You shall remember the LORD your God, for it is he who gives you power to get wealth, **that he may confirm his covenant that he swore to your fathers**, as it is this day.

   a. The discipline of the wilderness is training for entry into the Promised Land. No matter how blessed God's people become in the fullness of the promise, God never wants His people to forget that He redeemed them out of slavery when they had nothing and were oppressed.

   b. The training in the wilderness proves that God is all powerful and completely reliable even in the midst of snakes and scorpions and impossible conditions.

c. Once in the Promised Land, God warns not to become arrogant by forgetting that it was HE who gave all that was needed to prosper and not human strength or ability.
    i. This is why David's census was evil (2 Samuel 24, 1 Chronicles 21.) David counted the strength of his own army, exalting his fleshly power rather than the power of God. This is self-exaltation of human strength rather than faith in the Lord.

3. Deuteronomy 9:4-7 - 4 "**Do not say in your heart**, after the LORD your God has thrust them out before you, '**It is because of my righteousness** that the LORD has brought me in to possess this land,' whereas it is because of the wickedness of these nations that the LORD is driving them out before you. 5 **Not because of your righteousness or the uprightness of your heart are you going in to possess their land**, but because of the wickedness of these nations the LORD your God is driving them out from before you, **and that he may confirm the word that the LORD swore to your fathers, to Abraham, to Isaac, and to Jacob. 6 "Know, therefore, that the LORD your God is not giving you this good land to possess because of your righteousness, for you are a stubborn people. 7 Remember and do not forget how you provoked the LORD your God to wrath** in the wilderness. From the day you came out of the land of Egypt until you came to this place, you have been rebellious against the LORD.

    a. The wilderness trains us that it is not because of our righteousness because we are stubborn and rebellious and deserve nothing from God.
        i. As New Covenant believers, we learn that it is because of Jesus righteousness alone that we are blessed by God, not because of our obedience or goodness.

    b. The wilderness exposes our stubbornness, flesh, and rebellion against God. It is humiliating to appear unable to finish what God began or to enter into the fullness of His promise. But we are totally unable to do so on our own.
        i. The wilderness trains us in humility and lowliness. We gain an accurate understanding of ourselves and our own unworthiness of all the goodness God bestows upon us.

E. Wilderness 2: Tested as Sons

1. Luke 4:1-2 - 1 And Jesus, full of the Holy Spirit, returned from the Jordan and **was led by the Spirit in the wilderness** 2 **for forty days, being tempted by the devil**. And he ate nothing during those days. And when they were ended, he was hungry.

    a. The Spirit of the Lord led Jesus into the wilderness to be tested by the evil one.

        > Tempt/Test: Greek-G3985: peirazo: 1. To try whether a thing can be done. To scrutinize and examine. 2. To try or test for the purpose of ascertaining the quality of a person and how he thinks or how he will behave. 3. To maliciously or craftily test or put one to the proof. 4. To try or test one's faith, virtue, or character through enticement to sin.

    b. After forty days of fasting, Jesus was hungry.
        i. In our wilderness testing, it may take a while for us to drain out of our own strength enough for the testing to actually begin so that we may be tested to the fullest extent possible and proven in our faith.

2. Luke 4:3-4 - 3 The **devil said to him, "If you are the Son of God, command this stone to become bread."** 4 And Jesus answered him, **"It is written, 'Man shall not live by bread alone.'"**

   a. "IF" you are the Son of God is a test of identity in the heart. It is also a test of self-exaltation through the temptation to do something to prove ourselves rather than simply trust God.

   b. The test was to use the power of God to serve your stomach and indulge your flesh.
      i. Unlike Esau, Jesus' response was the equivalent of "I do not report to my stomach, I report to God – I am a disciplined Son."

   c. Jesus responded with the Word of God. "It is written." He kept Himself under the authority of Scripture and obeyed the commands of His Father.

3. Luke 4:5-8 - 5 And **the devil took him up and showed him all the kingdoms of the world in a moment of time**, 6 and said to him, "To you I will give all this authority and their glory, for it has been delivered to me, and I give it to whom I will. 7 **If you, then, will worship me, it will all be yours.**" 8 And Jesus answered him, **"It is written, 'You shall worship the Lord your God, and him only shall you serve.'"**

   a. Jesus was already slated to be King above all Kings – it was already His if He simply obeyed.
      i. Like the serpent promising Adam and Eve to be like God when they were already created in God's likeness.

   b. This is a temptation to take a shortcut by following the way of error rather than holding fast to the commands of God.
      i. Unlike Adam & Eve, Jesus responded with, "I do not report to you, I report to God – I am a disciplined Son."

4. Luke 4:9-12 - 9 And he took him to Jerusalem and set him on the pinnacle of the temple and said to him, "**If you are the Son of God, throw yourself down from here**, 10 **for it is written,** 'He will command his angels concerning you, to guard you,' 11 and 'On their hands they will bear you up, lest you strike your foot against a stone.'" 12 And Jesus answered him, "**It is said, 'You shall not put the Lord your God to the test.'**"

   > Note: In the Old Testament, people tested God through unbelief and actions of distrust, as if to test whether it was wise to distrust God and put faith in something else. Impious and wicked people through their evil conduct put God's justice and patience to the test.

   a. This is a test to not believe God or His timing by doing something self-exalting or performance driven. It is a test to force God's hand in displaying power for personal benefit.
      i. Jesus refused to step out of the will and timing of God. He was a disciplined Son.

   b. This a test to use spiritual power for show/display and to twist Scripture for selfish gain and self-advancement.
      i. Jesus refused to put God to the test or abuse the Word or power of God for illogical, high-risk activities that God did not author. He was a disciplined Son.

5. Luke 4:13 - 13 And when the devil had ended **every temptation**, he departed from him **until an opportune time.**

a. Jesus was tested ALL points but without sin. (Hebrews 4:15.) This was not only in the wilderness but in every facet of life, and even unto death.

b. We will be put to the test in every facet of life to prove whether or not we are sons of God, living and being led by the Holy Spirit. (Romans 8:15.)

6. Psalm 89:20-27 - 20 I have found David, my servant; with my holy oil I have anointed him, 21 so that my hand shall be established with him; my arm also shall strengthen him. 22 **The enemy shall not outwit him; the wicked shall not humble him.** 23 I will crush his foes before him and strike down those who hate him. 24 My faithfulness and my steadfast love shall be with him, and in my name shall his horn be exalted. 25 I will set his hand on the sea and his right hand on the rivers. 26 **He shall cry to me, 'You are my Father, my God, and the Rock of my salvation.'** 27 And **I will make him the firstborn**, the highest of the kings of the earth.

   a. Psalm 89 is about God's covenant faithfulness to David. This passage is not about David but David's offspring, the Messiah. (It was written after David had passed away.)

   b. The Son of David would not be outwitted by the enemy.

   > Outwit/Exact Usury: Hebrew-H5378: *nasa*: 1. To lend on interest or usury. To be a creditor. To dun/harass for debt.
   > Identical with: H5377: Beguile or deceive. Used by Eve in Genesis 3:13.

      i. The enemy outwitted/beguiled Adam and Eve into disobedience, putting them into debt to him under his rule. Because of this, all mankind is under the power of the devil. (1 John 5:19.)
         01. All of us have unpayable sin debts which require a ransom to be paid for our redemption to God.
      ii. Note: Jesus was never put into the enemy's debt, so no ransom was needed.
         01. In contrast, Jesus paid this ransom for us on the cross through His blood and death so that we can be sons of God.

   c. The Son of David would call God His Father and would be the firstborn of many brothers.
      i. Through our faith in Jesus and His blood which cleanses us from sin, the Holy Spirit comes to dwell inside of us and give us the same wisdom and strength that Jesus had as God's Son so that we will not be outwitted by the evil one. We can cry out to God as our "Abba, Father."

   d. Sons of God prove themselves by not being outwitted by the evil one and his many schemes of deception, by not acting on his counsel and being put into his debt. Instead, they cry out to God as their Father, and God helps them.

F. Take Up Your Cross & Follow Jesus

1. Get behind me Satan. Take up your cross.

   a. Matthew 16:21-24 - 21 From that time Jesus began to show his disciples that **he must go to Jerusalem and suffer many things from the elders and chief priests and scribes, and be killed**, and on the third day be raised. 22 And Peter took him aside and began to rebuke him, saying, "Far be it from you, Lord! **This shall never happen to you.**" 23 But he turned and said to Peter, "**Get behind me, Satan! You are a hindrance to me. For you are not setting your mind on the things of God, but on the things of man.**"

> Satan: Greek-G4567: *satanas*: 1. The devil. 2. Adversary. 3. The prince of evil spirits and enemy of God. 4. One who incites apostasy from God and to sin. *(abbreviated)*

      i. Well-intentioned friends might be speaking for the adversary of God, trying to lead you into sin and rebellion against God, whether they intend to or not.
      ii. Especially when trials come or God calls us to difficult things, or trials persist or grow in severity, they may say things like, "Surely God wouldn't want you to…"

  b. Matthew 16:24-26 - 24 Then Jesus told his disciples, "**If anyone would come after me, let him deny himself and take up his cross and follow me.** 25 For whoever would save his life will lose it, but whoever loses his life for my sake will find it. 26 For what will it profit a man if he gains the whole world and forfeits his soul? Or what shall a man give in return for his soul?

  c. Matthew 10:34-39 - 34 "Do not think that I have come to bring peace to the earth. I have not come to bring peace, but a sword. 35 For I have come to set a man against his father, and a daughter against her mother, and a daughter-in-law against her mother-in-law. 36 And a **person's enemies will be those of his own household**. 37 Whoever loves father or mother more than me is not worthy of me, and whoever loves son or daughter more than me is not worthy of me. 38 **And whoever does not take his cross and follow me is not worthy of me.** 39 **Whoever finds his life will lose it, and whoever loses his life for my sake will find it.**

2. It was God's will to crush Jesus. It is God's will for us to be crushed to our own will.

  a. Isaiah 53:10 - 10 **Yet it was the will of the LORD to crush him**; he has put him to grief; when his soul makes an offering for guilt, he shall see his offspring; he shall prolong his days; the will of the LORD shall prosper in his hand.
      i. It is the will of God for each and every follower of Jesus to live a life which follows the pattern of, "Not my will but yours be done." Our own will has to be crushed out of us completely.

  b. DO NOT avoid God's dealings and discipline in your life. Recognize the evil one speaking, even if it is through those who know and love if they have on their minds the ways of man.
      i. God wants us DEAD to ourselves so that we can be used by Him without our flesh and fantasies getting in the way.
      ii. It is ok to ask for another way but in the end, we must submit to the will of God.

3. No longer live for self or selfishness but for God.

  a. 2 Corinthians 5:15 - 15 and he died for all, **that those who live might no longer live for themselves but for him** who for their sake died and was raised.

  b. Galatians 2:20 - 20 **I have been crucified with Christ.** It is no longer I who live, but Christ who lives in me. And the life I now live in the flesh I live by faith in the Son of God, who loved me and gave himself for me.

  c. Galatians 5:24 - 24 And **those who belong to Christ Jesus have crucified the flesh** with its passions and desires.

d. Following Christ is a journey of total death to self, selfishness, and self-exaltation.

4. Crucified to this world.

    a. Galatians 6:14 - 14 But far be it from me to boast except in the cross of our Lord Jesus Christ, by which **the world has been crucified to me, and I to the world**.

    b. 1 John 2:16-17 - 16 For **all that is in the world--the desires of the flesh and the desires of the eyes and pride of life--is not from the Father but is from the world**. 17 And the world is passing away along with its desires, but whoever does the will of God abides forever.

    c. Unlike the Israelites in the wilderness always wanting to return to Egypt and calling Egypt the land of milk and honey because they forgot that they were slaves, we have to remain crucified to the world and the desires of this world as we take up our cross to follow Jesus.

5. Crucified to the promise, like Abraham, the father of the faithful:

    a. Abraham was tested through the offering of the one and only son who held the promise of God for a nation and people descended from Abraham to be blessed by God. Abraham was fully ready to put the knife into Isaac. He trusted God was able to fulfill His promise no matter what it looked like.

    b. We may be called upon to lay everything down on the altar of God – even the vision, ministry, calling, purpose, etc. that God has given us.
        i. Never be afraid to slay an Isaac – when in doubt, DIE to it by letting go, desisting of all self-effort and strength, and placing it entirely in God's hands.
        ii. Don't try, don't psychoanalyze, don't make excuses, don't blame shift, don't wiggle and squirm - just DIE to it.
        iii. God resurrects dead things. If you want God to move on something, DIE to it.

6. Jesus was like a lamb led to slaughter, offering no self-defense. He trusted that God would make Him victorious, even over death. He wants us to be the same way.

    a. Isaiah 53:7 - 7 He was oppressed, and he was afflicted, **yet he opened not his mouth; like a lamb that is led to the slaughter, and like a sheep that before its shearers is silent, so he opened not his mouth.**

    b. Jesus before the council of priests & elders:
        i. Matthew 26:62-65 - 62 And the high priest stood up and said, "Have you no answer to make? What is it that these men testify against you?" 63 **But Jesus remained silent**. And the high priest said to him, "I adjure you by the living God, tell us if you are the Christ, the Son of God." 64 Jesus said to him, "**You have said so. But I tell you, from now on you will see the Son of Man seated at the right hand of Power and coming on the clouds of heaven**." 65 Then the high priest tore his robes and said, "He has uttered blasphemy. What further witnesses do we need? You have now heard his blasphemy. (Also Mark 14:53-65; Luke 22:66-71.)

    c. Jesus before Pilate:
        i. Matthew 27:11-14 - 11 Now Jesus stood before the governor, and the governor asked him, "Are you the King of the Jews?" Jesus said, "You have said so." 12 **But when he was accused by the chief priests and elders, he gave no answer**. 13 Then Pilate said to him,

"Do you not hear how many things they testify against you?" 14 **But he gave him no answer, not even to a single charge**, so that the governor was greatly amazed. (Also Mark 15:2-5; Luke 23-:2-5.)

    ii. John 18:33-38 - 33 So Pilate entered his headquarters again and called Jesus and said to him, "Are you the King of the Jews?" 34 Jesus answered, "**Do you say this of your own accord, or did others say it to you about me?**" 35 Pilate answered, "Am I a Jew? Your own nation and the chief priests have delivered you over to me. What have you done?" 36 Jesus answered, "**My kingdom is not of this world. If my kingdom were of this world, my servants would have been fighting, that I might not be delivered over to the Jews. But my kingdom is not from the world.**" 37 Then Pilate said to him, "So you are a king?" Jesus answered, "**You say that I am a king. For this purpose I was born and for this purpose I have come into the world--to bear witness to the truth. Everyone who is of the truth listens to my voice.**" 38 Pilate said to him, "What is truth?" After he had said this, he went back outside to the Jews and told them, "I find no guilt in him.

    iii. John 19:9-11 - 9 He entered his headquarters again and said to Jesus, "Where are you from?" But **Jesus gave him no answer**. 10 So Pilate said to him, "You will not speak to me? Do you not know that I have authority to release you and authority to crucify you?" 11 Jesus answered him, "**You would have no authority over me at all unless it had been given you from above. Therefore he who delivered me over to you has the greater sin.**"

d. Jesus before Herod:
    i. Luke 23:8-11 - 8 When Herod saw Jesus, he was very glad, for he had long desired to see him, because he had heard about him, and he was hoping to see some sign done by him. 9 So he questioned him at some length, **but he made no answer**. 10 The chief priests and the scribes stood by, vehemently accusing him. 11 And Herod with his soldiers treated him with contempt and mocked him. Then, arraying him in splendid clothing, he sent him back to Pilate.

e. Jesus on the cross:
    i. Luke 23:33-34 - 33 And when they came to the place that is called The Skull, there they crucified him, and the criminals, one on his right and one on his left. 34 And Jesus said, "**Father, forgive them, for they know not what they do.**" And they cast lots to divide his garments.

7. Even if we seem like lambs led to slaughter in this world, we are more than conquerors, even over death, through Christ who was victorious over death and gives us eternal life!

    a. Romans 8:34-39 - 34 Who is to condemn? Christ Jesus is the one who died--more than that, who was raised--who is at the right hand of God, who indeed is interceding for us. 35 Who shall separate us from the love of Christ? Shall tribulation, or distress, or persecution, or famine, or nakedness, or danger, or sword? 36 **As it is written, "For your sake we are being killed all the day long; we are regarded as sheep to be slaughtered."** 37 **No, in all these things we are more than conquerors through him who loved us**. 38 For I am sure that neither death nor life, nor angels nor rulers, nor things present nor things to come, nor powers, 39 nor height nor depth, nor anything else in all creation, will be able to separate us from the love of God in Christ Jesus our Lord.

G. Learn by Observing the Trials of Others

1. The stories of Scripture are for our encouragement and endurance. We can learn from the failures and faithfulness of those in Scripture and have hope in God's faithfulness toward us.

    a. 1 Corinthians 10:11-13 - 11 **Now these things happened to them as an example, but they were written down for our instruction**, on whom the end of the ages has come. 12 Therefore let anyone who thinks that he stands take heed lest he fall. 13 **No temptation has overtaken you that is not common to man**. God is faithful, and he will not let you be tempted beyond your ability, but with the temptation he will also provide the way of escape, that you may be able to endure it.
        i. Don't be arrogant when reading the stories of Scripture just because you can turn the page and know how the story ends. Consider if you were in their position.
        ii. Be encouraged to learn the stories of God's faithfulness and blessings upon those who keep His way.

    b. Romans 15:4 - 4 For **whatever was written in former days was written for our instruction**, that through endurance and through the encouragement of the Scriptures we might have hope.

    c. James 5:10-11 - 10 **As an example of suffering and patience, brothers, take the prophets** who spoke in the name of the Lord. 11 Behold, we consider those blessed who remained steadfast. **You have heard of the steadfastness of Job**, and you have seen the purpose of the Lord, how the Lord is compassionate and merciful.

    d. 2 Timothy 3:16-17 - 16 **All Scripture is breathed out by God and profitable for teaching, for reproof, for correction, and for training in righteousness**, 17 that the man of God may be complete, equipped for every good work.

    e. Scripture supplies us with what we need to face our trials. So that we may say, "It is written," and have a clear word from God for each situation we face.

2. Consider your leaders and their outcome

    a. Hebrews 13:7-8 - 7 **Remember your leaders**, those who spoke to you the word of God. **Consider the outcome of their way of life**, and imitate their faith. 8 Jesus Christ is the same yesterday and today and forever.
        i. Leaders are under greater pressure and in the public eye. We may not always have the full story of what is going on behind the scenes, but the Lord can give us insight.
        ii. Leaders are called to a higher standard but are imperfect people. Sometimes they make wrong choices or are immoral or faithless. We can learn much from observing the results and consequences of their choices – both good and bad.

3. Consider the trials you witness others go through so that you do not repeat their errors.

    a. Jeremiah 3:6-11 - 6 The LORD said to me in the days of King Josiah: "Have you seen what she did, **that faithless one, Israel,** how she went up on every high hill and under every green tree, and there played the whore? 7 And I thought, 'After she has done all this she will return to me,' but she did not return, **and her treacherous sister Judah saw it.** 8 **She saw that for all the adulteries of that faithless one, Israel, I had sent her away with a decree of divorce. Yet her treacherous sister Judah did not fear, but she too went and played the whore.** 9 Because she took her whoredom lightly, she polluted the land, committing adultery with stone and tree.

10 **Yet for all this her treacherous sister Judah did not return to me with her whole heart, but in pretense**, declares the LORD." 11 And the LORD said to me, "Faithless Israel has shown herself more righteous than treacherous Judah.

    i. Judah saw Israel fall to Assyria but did not repent of their sins. Therefore, Judah fell to Babylon.

b. Daniel 5:18-23 - 18 O king, the Most High **God gave Nebuchadnezzar your father kingship and greatness and glory and majesty**. 19 And because of the greatness that he gave him, all peoples, nations, and languages trembled and feared before him. Whom he would, he killed, and whom he would, he kept alive; whom he would, he raised up, and whom he would, he humbled. 20 **But when his heart was lifted up and his spirit was hardened so that he dealt proudly, he was brought down from his kingly throne, and his glory was taken from him**. 21 He was driven from among the children of mankind, and his mind was made like that of a beast, and his dwelling was with the wild donkeys. He was fed grass like an ox, and his body was wet with the dew of heaven, **until he knew that the Most High God rules** the kingdom of mankind and sets over it whom he will. 22 **And you his son, Belshazzar, have not humbled your heart, though you knew all this**, 23 **but you have lifted up yourself against the Lord of heaven**. And the vessels of his house have been brought in before you, and you and your lords, your wives, and your concubines have drunk wine from them. And you have praised the gods of silver and gold, of bronze, iron, wood, and stone, which do not see or hear or know, but **the God in whose hand is your breath, and whose are all your ways, you have not honored**.

    i. Belshazzar saw the humiliation and restoration of Nebuchadnezzar but did not humble himself before God. He paid the price for this with his life.

Unit Eight: The Way to Salvation: Abide & Endure to the End

> For we have come to share in Christ, if indeed we hold our original confidence firm to the end.
> Hebrews 3:14

A. Abiding

1. Abiding in the Lord is an act of humbling ourselves because in order to abide in Jesus, we have to do things His way rather than our own.

   > Abide: Greek-G3306: *meno*: 1. To remain, abide. 2. To sojourn or tarry and not depart from, to continue to be present, to be kept or held continually. 3. To continue, not to perish, to last, to endure. 4. To remain as one and not become different.

2. John 15:1-17 - 1 "I am the true vine, and my Father is the vinedresser. 2 Every branch in me that does not bear fruit he takes away, and every branch that does bear fruit he prunes, that it may bear more fruit. 3 Already you are clean because of the word that I have spoken to you. 4 **Abide in me, and I in you. As the branch cannot bear fruit by itself, unless it abides in the vine, neither can you, unless you abide in me.** 5 **I am the vine; you are the branches. Whoever abides in me and I in him, he it is that bears much fruit, for apart from me you can do nothing**. 6 If anyone does not abide in me he is thrown away like a branch and withers; and the branches are gathered, thrown into the fire, and burned. 7 **If you abide in me, and my words abide in you, ask whatever you wish, and it will be done for you**. 8 By this my Father is glorified, that you bear much fruit and so prove to be my disciples. 9 As the Father has loved me, so have I loved you. **Abide in my love.** 10 **If you keep my commandments, you will abide in my love, just as I have kept my Father's commandments and abide in his love**. 11 These things I have spoken to you, that my joy may be in you, and that your joy may be full. 12 "**This is my commandment, that you love one another as I have loved you**. 13 Greater love has no one than this, that someone lay down his life for his friends. 14 **You are my friends if you do what I command you.** 15 No longer do I call you servants, for the servant does not know what his master is doing; but **I have called you friends, for all that I have heard from my Father I have made known to you**. 16 You did not choose me, but **I chose you and appointed you that you should go and bear fruit and that your fruit should abide**, so that whatever you ask the Father in my name, he may give it to you. 17 These things I command you, so that you will love one another.

3. We must remain in Jesus by obeying His commands, putting His teaching into practice, and bearing the fruit of His likeness.

   a. Galatians 5:22-23 - 22 But the **fruit of the Spirit** is love, joy, peace, patience, kindness, goodness, faithfulness, 23 gentleness, self-control; against such things there is no law.

   b. 2 Peter 1:5-10 - 5 For this very reason, **make every effort** to supplement your faith with virtue, and virtue with knowledge, 6 and knowledge with self-control, and self-control with steadfastness, and steadfastness with godliness, 7 and godliness with brotherly affection, and brotherly affection with love. 8 **For if these qualities are yours and are increasing, they keep you from being ineffective or unfruitful in the knowledge of our Lord Jesus Christ.** 9 For whoever lacks these qualities is so nearsighted that he is blind, having forgotten that he was cleansed from his former sins. 10 Therefore, brothers, **be all the more diligent to confirm your calling and election**, for if you practice these qualities you will never fall.

4. We must abide/continue in the faith in order to receive all that is promised.

    a. 1 Corinthians 15:1-2 - 1 Now I would remind you, brothers, of the gospel I preached to you, which you received, in which you stand, 2 and by which you are being saved, **if you hold fast to the word I preached to you--unless you believed in vain.**

    b. Romans 11:22 - 22 Note then the kindness and the severity of God: severity toward those who have fallen, but God's kindness to you, **provided you continue in his kindness. Otherwise you too will be cut off**.

    c. Hebrews 3:6, 14 - 6 but Christ is faithful over God's house as a son. And we are his house, **if indeed we hold fast our confidence and our boasting in our hope**. ... 14 For we have come to share in Christ, **if indeed we hold our original confidence firm to the end**.

B. Resting

1. Resting in the Lord is an act of humbling ourselves because it involves trusting God rather than our own efforts, work, labor, or strength.

2. The Sabbath is a sign between the Creator God and His people that He has redeemed them from slavery and the curse of sweat and toil to restore them to fellowship with Himself. The whole world is under the curse of sweat and toil. Working endlessly seems the best option for procuring the provision needed for survival. It takes great faith to take a day of REST unto the Lord, trusting that He is able to provide all that is needed.

    <u>Sabbath</u>: Hebrew-H7673: *sabat*: 1. To cease, desist, rest. 2. To desist from labor or exertion. 3. To put an end to. 4. To cause to cease, put an end to, etc.

    a. Sabbath was the first command God gave to Israel after they came out of Egyptian slavery. They had been redeemed from slavery, sweat, and toil to put their trust in God.
        i. Exodus 16:22-23 - 22 On the sixth day they gathered twice as much bread, two omers each. And when all the leaders of the congregation came and told Moses, 23 he said to them, "This is what the LORD has commanded: **'Tomorrow is a day of solemn rest, a holy Sabbath to the LORD**; bake what you will bake and boil what you will boil, and all that is left over lay aside to be kept till the morning.'"
        ii. Deuteronomy 5:15 - 15 You shall **remember that you were a slave in the land of Egypt**, and the LORD your God brought you out from there with a mighty hand and an outstretched arm. **Therefore the LORD your God commanded you to keep the Sabbath day.**

    b. Sabbath is a sign of sanctification and a sign of the relationship between Israel and the God who created all things.

- i. Exodus 31:13-17 - 13 "You are to speak to the people of Israel and say, **'Above all you shall keep my Sabbaths, for this is a sign between me and you throughout your generations, that you may know that I, the LORD, sanctify you**. 14 You shall keep the Sabbath, because it is holy for you. Everyone who profanes it shall be put to death. Whoever does any work on it, that soul shall be cut off from among his people. 15 **Six days shall work be done, but the seventh day is a Sabbath of solemn rest, holy to the LORD**. Whoever does any work on the Sabbath day shall be put to death. 16 Therefore the people of Israel shall keep the Sabbath, observing the Sabbath throughout their generations, as a covenant forever. 17 **It is a sign forever between me and the people of Israel that in six days the LORD made heaven and earth, and on the seventh day he rested and was refreshed.**"
    - 01. Anyone who violates the Sabbath was to be put to death. It is the equivalent of denying God's redemption.

- c. Sabbath is a day for honoring the Lord rather than seeking our own desires. It is a way of showing our delight in the Lord.
    - i. Isaiah 58:13-14 - 13 "**If you turn back your foot from the Sabbath, from doing your pleasure on my holy day, and call the Sabbath a delight and the holy day of the LORD honorable**; if you honor it, **not going your own ways, or seeking your own pleasure, or talking idly**; 14 then you shall take delight in the LORD, and I will make you ride on the heights of the earth; I will feed you with the heritage of Jacob your father, for the mouth of the LORD has spoken."

- d. Special Sabbaths were required at feast days, special times of year when the rest of the world was working over time to secure a good harvest, the people of God were commanded to rest and rejoice in the provision of God. (See Leviticus 23.)

- e. Note: We are not under Old Covenant Law to keep the Sabbath on Saturdays or the Feasts of the Lord. However, the importance of rest in God's sight should be noted.
    - i. To rest in the Lord remains an act of faith in His total redemption and provision for us.

3. In the New Covenant, Jesus gives us rest for our souls. We must strive to enter that rest through faith in what He did for us, redeeming us from sin and death.

    a. Matthew 11:28-30 - 28 **Come to me, all who labor and are heavy laden, and I will give you rest**. 29 Take my yoke upon you, and learn from me, for I am gentle and lowly in heart, and **you will find rest for your souls**. 30 For my yoke is easy, and my burden is light."
    - i. Jesus paid for our total redemption, sanctification, and for us to stand righteous before God through faith in Him.
    - ii. Jesus gives us rest from all religious activity trying to earn or deserve right standing before God. His yoke is easy because He lived the life we could never live and paid the full price for us to be reckoned as righteous in God's sight.

    b. Hebrews 4:1-11 - 1 Therefore, while **the promise of entering his rest still stands, let us fear lest any of you should seem to have failed to reach it**. 2 For good news came to us just as to them, but the message they heard did not benefit them, because they were not united by faith with those who listened. 3 For **we who have believed enter that rest**, as he has said, "As I swore in my wrath, 'They shall not enter my rest,'" although his works were finished from the foundation of the world. 4 For he has somewhere spoken of the seventh day in this way: "And God rested on the seventh day from all his works." 5 And again in this passage he said, "They shall not enter my rest." 6 Since therefore it remains for some to enter it, and **those who formerly received the

good news failed to enter because of disobedience, 7 again he appoints a certain day, "Today," saying through David so long afterward, in the words already quoted, "**Today, if you hear his voice, do not harden your hearts.**" 8 For if Joshua had given them rest, God would not have spoken of another day later on. 9 **So then, there remains a Sabbath rest for the people of God,** 10 **for whoever has entered God's rest has also rested from his works as God did from his.** 11 **Let us therefore strive to enter that rest, so that no one may fall by the same sort of disobedience.**

- i. Hebrew/Jewish believers were considering forsaking Jesus to return to the Law of Moses because persecution had gone on so long and Jesus had not yet returned. Returning to observing the Old Covenant commands for the purpose of attaining right standing with God is denying the redemption of Jesus.
    - 01. Galatians 5:4 - 4 You are severed from Christ, **you who would be justified by the law; you have fallen away from grace**.
- ii. Righteousness is attained in the New Covenant by grace through faith.
    - 01. Ephesians 2:8-9 - 8 For by grace you have been saved through faith. **And this is not your own doing; it is the gift of God**, 9 **not a result of works**, so that no one may boast.

4. Jesus Himself often withdrew to desolate places to rest and pray. He led His disciples into this type of rest as well.

    a. Mark 6:30-32 - 30 The apostles returned to Jesus and told him all that they had done and taught. 31 And he said to them, "**Come away by yourselves to a desolate place and rest a while.**" For many were coming and going, and they had no leisure even to eat. 32 And they went away in the boat to a desolate place by themselves.

    b. Jesus withdrew for rest and prayer BEFORE and AFTER significant ministry events to receive guidance, refreshment, and strength from the Father. He did nothing in His own strength but constantly sought the supply of strength from heaven.

C. Waiting Upon the Lord

1. Waiting upon the Lord subjects us to God and His timing. We are His servants, looking to Him and not doing anything of our own accord or out of our own sensibilities.

    a. Psalm 123:2 - 2 Behold, **as the eyes of servants look to the hand of their master, as the eyes of a maidservant to the hand of her mistress**, so our eyes look to the LORD our God, till he has mercy upon us.
    - i. A servant has no individuality or purpose other than to serve their master. A maidservant's entire life is devoted to serving the needs and desires of her lady
    - ii. It is not for a servant to do whatever they please, on their own time, or for their own benefit. Everything they do is according to the will of their master.

2. Waiting upon the Lord is an act of denying ourselves of our own will and desire to press forward with activity. Activity might make us feel useful, productive, or important but if it is not authored by God or done in God's timing, it can do more harm than good.

    a. Psalm 37:7-9, 34 - 7 **Be still before the LORD and wait patiently for him**; fret not yourself over the one who prospers in his way, over the man who carries out evil devices! 8 Refrain from anger, and forsake wrath! Fret not yourself; it tends only to evil. 9 For the evildoers shall be cut off, but **those who wait for the LORD shall inherit the land.** ... 34 **Wait for the LORD and keep his way, and he will exalt you to inherit the land**; you will look on when the wicked are cut off.

   b. Psalm 130:5-6 - 5 **I wait for the LORD, my soul waits**, and in his word I hope; 6 **my soul waits for the Lord more than watchmen for the morning**, more than watchmen for the morning.
      i. Note: Watchmen wait all through the night for the slightest hint of dawn.

   c. Isaiah 64:4 - 4 From of old no one has heard or perceived by the ear, no eye has seen a God besides you, who acts for those who wait for him.

   d. Exodus 14:14 NIV - 14 The LORD will fight for you; **you need only to be still**.

3. We must wait for the Lord for the fulfillment of prophetic vision.

   a. Habakkuk 2:2-4 - 2 And the LORD answered me: "Write the vision; make it plain on tablets, so he may run who reads it. 3 For still **the vision awaits its appointed time; it hastens to the end--it will not lie. If it seems slow, wait for it; it will surely come; it will not delay.** 4 "Behold, his soul is puffed up; it is not upright within him, but **the righteous shall live by his faith.**
      i. Even if the vision seems delayed, in its time, it will not be delayed.
      ii. The proud are puffed up and live by their own devices. The righteous live by faith.

   b. Example: Abraham with Ishmael & Isaac. After years of waiting for God to give him a son in fulfillment of his promise, Abraham succumbed to a plan concocted by his wife, Sarah. The plan was for her servant, Hagar, to conceive a child for Abraham in Sarah's name. From this, Ishmael was born. Eventually, God returned and promised that Sarah would have a son and his name was to be Isaac. It was Isaac who fulfilled the promise of God. Abraham loved Ishmael and it broke his heart that Ishmael could not be blessed by God. Eventually, Ishmael persecuted Isaac and had to be sent away completely which was even more upsetting to Abraham. (See Genesis 17, 21.)
      i. Genesis 17:18-21 - 18 And Abraham said to God, "**Oh that Ishmael might live before you!**" 19 **God said, "No**, but Sarah your wife shall bear you a son, and you shall call his name Isaac. I will establish my covenant with him as an everlasting covenant for his offspring after him. 20 As for Ishmael, I have heard you; behold, I have blessed him and will make him fruitful and multiply him greatly. He shall father twelve princes, and I will make him into a great nation. 21 **But I will establish my covenant with Isaac**, whom Sarah shall bear to you at this time next year."
      ii. Galatians 4:22-23, 29-30 - 22 For it is written that Abraham had two sons, one by a slave woman and one by a free woman. 23 But **the son of the slave was born according to the flesh, while the son of the free woman was born through promise**. ... 29 But just as at that time **he who was born according to the flesh persecuted him who was born according to the Spirit**, so also it is now. 30 But what does the Scripture say? "Cast out the slave woman and her son, for the son of the slave woman shall not inherit with the son of the free woman."

   c. Example: Joseph's dream. Joseph had a dream that his brothers would all bow down to him. Joseph announced this to his family and Jacob took note of it. Joseph was sold by his brothers into slavery, became a slave of Potiphar, was falsely accused by Potiphar's wife and was thrown into prison. From prison, he interpreted dreams for fellow prisoners, asking

them to remember him when they were released but it was two more years before the fullness of time for Joseph to stand before Pharaoh and see the vision fulfilled.
   i. Genesis 37:11 - 11 And his brothers were jealous of him, but **his father kept the saying in mind**.
   ii. Genesis 45:4-8 - 4 So Joseph said to his brothers, "Come near to me, please." And they came near. And he said, "**I am your brother, Joseph, whom you sold into Egypt**. 5 And now do not be distressed or angry with yourselves because you sold me here, for **God sent me before you to preserve life**. 6 For the famine has been in the land these two years, and there are yet five years in which there will be neither plowing nor harvest. 7 And **God sent me before you to preserve for you a remnant on earth, and to keep alive for you many survivors**. 8 **So it was not you who sent me here, but God**. He has made me a father to Pharaoh, and lord of all his house and ruler over all the land of Egypt.
   iii. Psalm 105:16-19 - 16 When he summoned a famine on the land and broke all supply of bread, 17 he had sent a man ahead of them, Joseph, who was sold as a slave. 18 His feet were hurt with fetters; his neck was put in a collar of iron; 19 **until what he had said came to pass, the word of the LORD tested him**.

d. Example: David's kingship. David was anointed by Samuel to be King of Israel when he was a shepherd boy many years before he became king of all Israel. He served faithfully in Saul's kingdom until he had to flee for his life because Saul was trying to kill him. After fleeing, David lived as a fugitive in caves, in the wilderness, and in enemy territory while still honoring Saul as God's appointed king in Israel. Eventually, Saul took his own life and David was appointed King over Judah. Then, seven years later, he was appointed King over all Israel.
   i. 1 Samuel 16:12-13 - 12 And he sent and brought him in. Now he was ruddy and had beautiful eyes and was handsome. And the LORD said, "Arise, anoint him, for this is he." 13 **Then Samuel took the horn of oil and anointed him in the midst of his brothers**. And the Spirit of the LORD rushed upon David from that day forward. And Samuel rose up and went to Ramah.
   ii. 2 Samuel 2:4 - 4 And **the men of Judah came, and there they anointed David king over the house of Judah**. When they told David, "It was the men of Jabesh-gilead who buried Saul,"
   iii. 2 Samuel 5:3-5 - 3 **So all the elders of Israel came** to the king at Hebron, and King David made a covenant with them at Hebron before the LORD, and **they anointed David king over Israel**. 4 David was thirty years old when he began to reign, and he reigned forty years. 5 **At Hebron he reigned over Judah seven years and six months, and at Jerusalem he reigned over all Israel and Judah thirty-three years.**

e. Example John the Baptist in the wilderness. The call of God on the life of John the Baptist was known from before he was conceived. Nevertheless,
   i. Luke 1:16-17 - 16 And he will turn many of the children of Israel to the Lord their God, 17 **and he will go before him in the spirit and power of Elijah**, to turn the hearts of the fathers to the children, and the disobedient to the wisdom of the just, **to make ready for the Lord a people prepared**."
   ii. Luke 1:76-80 - 76 **And you, child, will be called the prophet of the Most High; for you will go before the Lord to prepare his ways**, 77 to give knowledge of salvation to his people in the forgiveness of their sins, 78 because of the tender mercy of our God, whereby the sunrise shall visit us from on high 79 to give light to those who sit in darkness and in the shadow of death, to guide our feet into the way of peace." 80 **And the child grew and became strong in spirit**, and **he was in the wilderness until the day of his public appearance to Israel.**

-
  -
    - iii. Luke 3:1-3 - 1 In the fifteenth year of the reign of Tiberius Caesar, Pontius Pilate being governor of Judea, and Herod being tetrarch of Galilee, and his brother Philip tetrarch of the region of Ituraea and Trachonitis, and Lysanias tetrarch of Abilene, 2 **during the high priesthood of Annas and Caiaphas, the word of God came to John the son of Zechariah in the wilderness.** 3 **And he went into all the region around the Jordan, proclaiming a baptism of repentance for the forgiveness of sins.**

  - f. Example: Jesus with His parents. Jesus was ready by age twelve in maturity and wisdom to stand before the religious leaders and refute them. But He waited eighteen more years, submitting under the authority of His parents, until the time came for Him to begin ministry.
    - i. Luke 2:42, 46-52 - 42 And **when he was twelve years old**, they went up according to custom. ... 46 After three days **they found him in the temple, sitting among the teachers, listening to them and asking them questions.** 47 **And all who heard him were amazed at his understanding and his answers.** 48 And when his parents saw him, they were astonished. And his mother said to him, "Son, why have you treated us so? Behold, your father and I have been searching for you in great distress." 49 And he said to them, "Why were you looking for me? Did you not know that I must be in my Father's house?" 50 And they did not understand the saying that he spoke to them. 51 **And he went down with them and came to Nazareth and was submissive to them.** And his mother treasured up all these things in her heart. 52 **And Jesus increased in wisdom and in stature and in favor with God and man.**

4. Waiting like servants for their Master to return.

   a. Luke 12:35-36 - 35 Stay dressed for action and keep your lamps burning, 36 and **be like men who are waiting for their master to come home** from the wedding feast, so that they may open the door to him at once when he comes and knocks.

   b. In the end times, there will be tremendous pressure from every side to bow to the forces of this world, to take matters into our own hands, and to stop waiting upon the Lord. It will seem irresponsible, illogical, impractical and foolish to wait for the Lord. But we will be blessed for not bowing our knee to anything or anyone other than Jesus Himself.
      - i. Note: This is part of why practicing the discipline of waiting upon the Lord is so important in our daily lives. If we train ourselves to wait upon the Lord and only move when He moves, it will come easily to us when the pressures intensify.

   c. James 5:7-8 - 7 **Be patient, therefore, brothers, until the coming of the Lord.** See how the farmer waits for the precious fruit of the earth, being patient about it, until it receives the early and the late rains. 8 **You also, be patient. Establish your hearts**, for the coming of the Lord is at hand.

5. Those who wait upon the Lord will be rewarded and will receive what God promised.

   a. Isaiah 40:30-31 - 30 Even youths shall faint and be weary, and young men shall fall exhausted; but **they who wait for the LORD shall renew their strength**; they shall mount up with wings like eagles; they shall run and not be weary; they shall walk and not faint.

   b. Psalm 27:13-14 - 13 I believe that **I shall look upon the goodness of the LORD in the land of the living!** 14 **Wait for the LORD**; be strong, and let your heart take courage; **wait for the LORD!**

c. Psalm 40:1-4 - 1 **I waited patiently for the LORD; he inclined to me and heard my cry.** 2 He drew me up from the pit of destruction, out of the miry bog, and set my feet upon a rock, making my steps secure. 3 He put a new song in my mouth, a song of praise to our God. Many will see and fear, and put their trust in the LORD. 4 **Blessed is the man who makes the LORD his trust, who does not turn to the proud, to those who go astray after a lie!**

D. Not Presuming or Taking Matters into Our Own Hands

1. We must not be presumptuous and take the matters of God into our own hands, even under intense pressure from enemies or from other people.

   a. Proverbs 16:25 - 25 **There is a way that seems right to a man**, but its end is the way to death.

   b. Even if something is revealed to us by God, we must wait for God's timing rather than trying to step into it prematurely or out of season.

2. Example: Moses. Moses was raised in Pharaoh's palace in all the ways of Egypt. But at some point, he came to understand his calling as the deliverer of God's people in His generation. At first, he took matters into his own hands trying to exert authority over the Hebrew slaves because he presumed that they would recognize God's call upon his life. They did not. After this, Moses fled into the wilderness for forty years until the time came when God called him into service. (See also, Exodus 2-3.)

   a. Acts 7:23-36 - 23 "When he was forty years old, it came into his heart to visit his brothers, the children of Israel. 24 And seeing one of them being wronged, he defended the oppressed man and avenged him by striking down the Egyptian. 25 **He supposed that his brothers would understand that God was giving them salvation by his hand, but they did not understand.** 26 And on the following day he appeared to them as they were quarreling and tried to reconcile them, saying, 'Men, you are brothers. Why do you wrong each other?' 27 But the man who was wronging his neighbor thrust him aside, saying, 'Who made you a ruler and a judge over us? 28 Do you want to kill me as you killed the Egyptian yesterday?' 29 **At this retort Moses fled and became an exile in the land of Midian**, where he became the father of two sons. 30 "**Now when forty years had passed, an angel appeared to him in the wilderness of Mount Sinai, in a flame of fire in a bush.** 31 When Moses saw it, he was amazed at the sight, and as he drew near to look, there came the voice of the Lord: 32 'I am the God of your fathers, the God of Abraham and of Isaac and of Jacob.' And Moses trembled and did not dare to look. 33 **Then the Lord said to him, 'Take off the sandals from your feet, for the place where you are standing is holy ground.** 34 I have surely seen the affliction of my people who are in Egypt, and have heard their groaning, and I have come down to deliver them. **And now come, I will send you to Egypt.'** 35 "**This Moses, whom they rejected, saying, 'Who made you a ruler and a judge?'--this man God sent as both ruler and redeemer by the hand of the angel who appeared to him in the bush.** 36 This man led them out, performing wonders and signs in Egypt and at the Red Sea and in the wilderness for forty years.

3. Example: Promised Land Presumption. When the twelve spies returned from the Promised Land with a bounty of the Land's goodness, they came with a bad report filled with doubt and unbelief that God would not be able to deliver the Land to them as He had promised. Only Joshua and Caleb believed that God would be faithful to fight for them. The people agreed with the bad report and refused to go into battle to take possession of the Land. Therefore, God

ordered that the entire generation of people twenty years old and older would perish in the wilderness because they did not believe. After hearing this, they attempted to take the Land for themselves in their own strength, even though Moses told them that the Lord was not with them. They were chased out by the enemy as if by a swarm of bees to their utter humiliation. (See also Numbers 13-14.)

   a. Deuteronomy 1:41-45 - 41 "Then you answered me, 'We have sinned against the LORD. **We ourselves will go up and fight**, just as the LORD our God commanded us.' And every one of you fastened on his weapons of war and thought it easy to go up into the hill country. 42 And the LORD said to me, '**Say to them, Do not go up or fight, for I am not in your midst, lest you be defeated before your enemies**.' 43 So I spoke to you, and **you would not listen; but you rebelled against the command of the LORD and presumptuously went up** into the hill country. 44 Then the Amorites who lived in that hill country came out against you and **chased you as bees do and beat you down** in Seir as far as Hormah. 45 And you returned and wept before the LORD, but the LORD did not listen to your voice or give ear to you.

4. Example: King Saul: Instance #1. Samuel told King Saul to wait seven days for him to arrive at Gilgal in order for Samuel to offer sacrifices to the Lord for the impending battle against the Philistines. Saul waited seven days but when it did not seem that Samuel was coming and the pressure of battle was mounting and people were starting to scatter from Saul, he offered the sacrifices himself, which a king is not authorized to do. For this, the Kingdom was removed from Saul and God sought a man after His heart not their own heart.

   a. 1 Samuel 13:11-14 - 11 Samuel said, "What have you done?" And Saul said, "**When I saw that the people were scattering from me, and that you did not come within the days appointed, and that the Philistines had mustered** at Michmash, 12 I said, 'Now the Philistines will come down against me at Gilgal, and **I have not sought the favor of the LORD.' So I forced myself, and offered the burnt offering**." 13 And Samuel said to Saul, "You have done foolishly. You have not kept the command of the LORD your God, with which he commanded you. For then the LORD would have established your kingdom over Israel forever. 14 But now your kingdom shall not continue. **The LORD has sought out a man after his own heart**, and the LORD has commanded him to be prince over his people, because you have not kept what the LORD commanded you."

5. Example: King Saul: Instance #2. Shortly after this first incident, Saul was commanded to devote the Amalekites to total destruction. Instead of obeying the commands of the Lord, he caved into pressure from the people. He failed to kill the king of the Amalekites, and instead of devoting the spoils to destruction, brought them to the Lord for sacrifice.

   a. 1 Samuel 15:19-24 - 19 **Why then did you not obey the voice of the LORD? Why did you pounce on the spoil and do what was evil in the sight of the LORD?**" 20 And Saul said to Samuel, "I have obeyed the voice of the LORD. I have gone on the mission on which the LORD sent me. I have brought Agag the king of Amalek, and I have devoted the Amalekites to destruction. 21 **But the people took of the spoil, sheep and oxen, the best of the things devoted to destruction, to sacrifice to the LORD your God** in Gilgal." 22 And Samuel said, "**Has the LORD as great delight in burnt offerings and sacrifices, as in obeying the voice of the LORD? Behold, to obey is better than sacrifice, and to listen than the fat of rams**. 23 **For rebellion is as the sin of divination, and presumption is as iniquity and idolatry**. Because you have rejected the word of the LORD, he has also rejected you from being king." 24 Saul said to Samuel, "I have sinned, for I have transgressed the commandment of the LORD and your words, **because I feared the people and obeyed their voice**.

i. Obedience is more valuable to God than action based on our own ideas of what is pleasing to Him. Listening to Him is better than offering rams.
ii. Taking matters into our own hands is rebellion against God.
iii. Presumption is equivalent to idolatry in God's sight. The idol is ourselves.

6. Not presuming upon the grace of God to indulge in sin and error.

    a. Romans 2:4 - 4 Or **do you presume on the riches of his kindness and forbearance and patience, not knowing that God's kindness is meant to lead you to repentance?**
        i. God's grace and mercy are not a license for sin and lawlessness, indulging our own lusts and doing things our own way.

E. Enduring to the End

1. The trials we go through will test our willingness to deny ourselves, suffer for Jesus, and persevere in His ways rather than giving way to temptation or caving into pressures of man, need, or desire.

    a. Matthew 24:9-13 - 9 "**Then they will deliver you up to tribulation and put you to death, and you will be hated by all nations for my name's sake**. 10 And then **many will fall away** and betray one another and hate one another. 11 And many false prophets will arise and lead many astray. 12 And because lawlessness will be increased, the love of many will grow cold. 13 **But the one who endures to the end will be saved.**

    b. Hebrews 10:35-39 - 35 Therefore **do not throw away your confidence**, which has a great reward. 36 For **you have need of endurance**, so that when you have done the will of God you may receive what is promised. 37 For, "Yet a little while, and the coming one will come and will not delay; 38 but my righteous one shall live by faith, and **if he shrinks back, my soul has no pleasure in him.**" 39 **But we are not of those who shrink back and are destroyed, but of those who have faith and preserve their souls.**

    c. Revelation 12:10-11 - 10 And I heard a loud voice in heaven, saying, "**Now the salvation and the power and the kingdom of our God and the authority of his Christ have come**, for the accuser of our brothers has been thrown down, who accuses them day and night before our God. 11 **And they have conquered him by the blood of the Lamb and by the word of their testimony, for they loved not their lives even unto death.**

Unit Nine: The Way of Christ: Meekness & Sonship

> Blessed are the meek, for they shall inherit the earth.
> Matthew 5:5

A. Meekness

1. Blessed are the meek.

    a. Matthew 5:5 - 5 **Blessed are the meek**, for they shall inherit the earth.

    > Meek: Greek-G4239: *praus*: 1. Mildness of disposition, gentleness of spirit. 2. Humble.

    > *Notes from Biblical Usage:* Meekness toward God is that disposition of spirit in which we accept His dealings with us as good, and therefore without disputing or resisting. In the OT, the meek are those wholly relying on God rather than their own strength to defend against injustice. Thus, meekness toward evil people means knowing God is permitting the injuries they inflict, that He is using them to purify His elect, and that He will deliver His elect in His time. Gentleness or meekness is the opposite to self-assertiveness and self-interest. It stems from trust in God's goodness and control over the situation. The gentle person is not occupied with self at all. This is a work of the Holy Spirit, not of the human will.

      i. 1 Peter 3:4 - 4 but let your adorning be the hidden person of the heart with **the imperishable beauty of a gentle [meek] and quiet spirit**, which in God's sight is very precious.
      ii. Ephesians 4:1-2 - 1 I therefore, a prisoner for the Lord, urge you to **walk in a manner worthy of the calling to which you have been called**, 2 **with all humility [lowliness] and gentleness [meekness]**, with patience, bearing with one another in love,

    b. Psalm 37:7-11 - 7 **Be still before the LORD and wait patiently for him**; fret not yourself over the one who prospers in his way, over the man who carries out evil devices! 8 **Refrain from anger, and forsake wrath!** Fret not yourself; it tends only to evil. 9 For the evildoers shall be cut off, but **those who wait for the LORD shall inherit the land**. 10 In just a little while, the wicked will be no more; though you look carefully at his place, he will not be there. 11 **But the meek shall inherit the land and delight themselves in abundant peace.**

    > Meek: Hebrew-H6035: *anav*: 1. Poor, humble, gentle, afflicted – with the notion of a lowly, pious, and modest mind which prefers to bear injuries rather than return them. 2. Weak, needy, lowly. 3. Oppressed by the rich and powerful.

2. Jesus was meek.

    a. Matthew 11:29 KJV - 29 Take my yoke upon you, and learn of me; for **I am meek and lowly in heart**: and ye shall find rest unto your souls.

b. Isaiah 42:1-3 - 1 Behold my servant, whom I uphold, my chosen, in whom my soul delights; I have put my Spirit upon him; he will bring forth justice to the nations. 2 **He will not cry aloud or lift up his voice**, or make it heard in the street; 3 **a bruised reed he will not break, and a faintly burning wick he will not quench**; he will faithfully bring forth justice.

c. Matthew 21:5 - 5 "Say to the daughter of Zion, 'Behold, **your king is coming to you, humble [meek]**, and mounted on a donkey, on a colt, the foal of a beast of burden.'"

d. Isaiah 53:7-9 - 7 **He was oppressed, and he was afflicted, yet he opened not his mouth**; like a lamb that is led to the slaughter, and like a sheep that before its shearers is silent, so he opened not his mouth. 8 **By oppression and judgment he was taken away**; and as for his generation, who considered that he was cut off out of the land of the living, stricken for the transgression of my people? 9 And they made his grave with the wicked and with a rich man in his death, **although he had done no violence, and there was no deceit in his mouth**.

e. 1 Peter 2:23 - 23 **When he was reviled, he did not revile in return**; when he suffered, he did not threaten, but **continued entrusting himself to him who judges justly**.

3. True meekness includes boldness for purity without compromise.

   a. James 3:17 - 17 But the **wisdom from above is first pure, then peaceable**, gentle, open to reason, full of mercy and good fruits, impartial and sincere.
      i. Jesus went to the cross, allowing Himself to be overruled by evil, rather than diminish or compromise the purity of the truth.

   b. Acts 4:29-31 - 29 And now, Lord, **look upon their threats and grant to your servants to continue to speak your word with all boldness**, 30 while you stretch out your hand to heal, and signs and wonders are performed through the name of your holy servant Jesus." 31 And when they had prayed, the place in which they were gathered together was shaken, and they were all filled with the Holy Spirit **and continued to speak the word of God with boldness**.
      i. The early church believers prayed for boldness to not compromise the message of Christ even in the midst of severe persecution and threat of death.

4. Meekness is not weakness in the face of religious people and their error.

   a. Example: John the Baptist was a man submitted to God and filled with fire and boldness to prepare Israel for the coming Messiah, particularly confronting the religious leaders.
      i. Matthew 3:7-8 - 7 But **when he saw many of the Pharisees and Sadducees** coming to his baptism, he said to them, "**You brood of vipers!** Who warned you to flee from the wrath to come? 8 Bear fruit in keeping with repentance.
      ii. Matthew 11:7-10 - 7 As they went away, Jesus began to speak to the crowds concerning John [the Baptist]: "**What did you go out into the wilderness to see? A reed shaken by the wind? 8 What then did you go out to see? A man dressed in soft clothing?** Behold, those who wear soft clothing are in kings' houses. 9 What then did you go out to see? A prophet? Yes, I tell you, and more than a prophet. 10 This is he of whom it is written, "'Behold, I send my messenger before your face, who will prepare your way before you.'
         01. A shaking reed or softly clothed man suggests something flimsy and easily given to self-indulgence.

   b. Example: Jesus questioned when He was struck improperly by the High Priest's officer.

i. John 18:23 - 23 Jesus answered him, "If what I said is wrong, bear witness about the wrong; **but if what I said is right, why do you strike me?**"

c. Example: Paul retorted when he was struck improperly by the High Priest's officer but then retracted his insult when he learned that it was the High Priest.
   i. Acts 23:3-5 - 3 Then Paul said to him, "**God is going to strike you, you whitewashed wall! Are you sitting to judge me according to the law, and yet contrary to the law you order me to be struck?**" 4 Those who stood by said, "Would you revile God's high priest?" 5 And Paul said, "I did not know, brothers, that he was the high priest, for it is written, '**You shall not speak evil of a ruler of your people.**'"

B. Childlikeness: Becoming Like a Child

1. Matthew 18:1-4 - 1 At that time the disciples came to Jesus, saying, "Who is the greatest in the kingdom of heaven?" 2 And **calling to him a child**, he put him in the midst of them 3 and said, "Truly, I say to you, **unless you turn and become like children, you will never enter the kingdom of heaven**. 4 Whoever humbles himself like this child is the greatest in the kingdom of heaven.

   a. A child is totally dependent on another more mature person to care for them, provide for them, guide them, protect them, and show them the way they should go.

   b. A child is uncomplicated and without complex plans and schemes.

   c. A child is teachable and submissive because they do not presume that they know better.

   d. A child forgives easily and moves on easily without holding a grudge.

2. Luke 10:21 - 21 In that same hour he rejoiced in the Holy Spirit and said, "I thank you, Father, Lord of heaven and earth, that **you have hidden these things from the wise and understanding and revealed them to little children; yes, Father, for such was your gracious will.**

   a. Jesus rejoiced over God's will being revealed to those who were simple enough to believe it.

   b. Psalm 8:2 - 2 **Out of the mouth of babies and infants**, you have established strength because of your foes, to still the enemy and the avenger.
      i. God proves Himself mighty on behalf of those who hope in Him.

3. God is glorified through our childlikeness/weakness.

   a. 1 Corinthians 1:26-29 - 26 For consider your calling, brothers: not many of you were wise according to worldly standards, not many were powerful, not many were of noble birth. 27 But **God chose what is foolish in the world** to shame the wise; **God chose what is weak in the world** to shame the strong; 28 **God chose what is low and despised in the world, even things that are not**, to bring to nothing things that are, 29 so that no human being might boast in the presence of God.

   b. 2 Corinthians 4:7 - 7 But **we have this treasure in jars of clay**, to show that the surpassing power belongs to God and not to us.

C. Mature Sonship: The Likeness of God as Revealed in Jesus

1. Jesus is the exact likeness of God in human form.

   a. Hebrews 1:1-3a - 1 Long ago, at many times and in many ways, God spoke to our fathers by the prophets, 2 **but in these last days he has spoken to us by his Son**, whom he appointed the heir of all things, through whom also he created the world. 3 **He is the radiance of the glory of God and the exact imprint of his nature**, and he upholds the universe by the word of his power.
      i. Prophets were spokesmen for God but with human nature, including frailties and failures. Jesus is the Son of God with perfect divine nature and without sin.

   b. Colossians 1:15 - 15 **He is the image of the invisible God**, the firstborn of all creation.

   c. Biblical transparency is to see God clearly. Jesus was perfectly transparent so that the nature of God was shown through Him.
      i. Example: On a projector, a transparency is used to project an image on a screen. Anything on the transparency will be magnified when the light of the projector shines through it. Jesus was so transparent that there were no obstructions or markings to block or hinder the light of God shining through Him completely. In everything He did, He did the will of God completely. This is Biblical transparency and the type of transparency we are called to as followers of Jesus.
      ii. Psychology uses the term "transparent" in regard to being open about our faults, failures, desires, and motives so that we are not hidden or two-faced. This is the wisdom of man.

2. We have been adopted as sons/children of God to reflect His likeness to the world and shine brightly as lights for Him to the world.

   a. Romans 8:13-17 - 13 For if you live according to the flesh you will die, but **if by the Spirit you put to death the deeds of the body**, you will live. 14 For **all who are led by the Spirit of God are sons of God**. 15 For you did not receive the spirit of slavery to fall back into fear, but you have **received the Spirit of adoption as sons, by whom we cry, "Abba! Father!"** 16 The **Spirit himself bears witness with our spirit that we are children of God**, 17 and if children, then heirs-- heirs of God and fellow heirs with Christ, **provided we suffer with him in order that we may also be glorified with him**.
      i. We are only sons of God if we are led by the Spirit of God in order to reflect the nature of God.
      ii. What we suffer for and how we respond to suffering proves whether or not we are being led by the Holy Spirit.

   b. 2 Peter 1:3-4 - 3 **His divine power has granted to us all things that pertain to life and godliness**, through the knowledge of him who called us to his own glory and excellence, 4 by which he has granted to us his precious and very great promises, so that through them you may **become partakers of the divine nature, having escaped from the corruption that is in the world because of sinful desire**.
      i. Godliness is God-likeness. We participate with divine nature by the indwelling Holy Spirit to become more and more like God.

3. If we continue to indulge our flesh, we show ourselves to be sons of disobedience like the world and sons of the evil one.

a. 1 John 3:9-10 - 9 **No one born of God makes a practice of sinning**, for God's seed abides in him; and he cannot keep on sinning, because he has been born of God. 10 **By this it is evident who are the children of God, and who are the children of the devil**: whoever does not practice righteousness is not of God, nor is the one who does not love his brother.

D. Submission & Slavery to God

1. We are called to lay our lives down as a living sacrifice to God.

    a. Hebrews 10:5-7 - 5 Consequently, when Christ came into the world, he said, "Sacrifices and offerings you have not desired, **but a body have you prepared for me**; 6 in burnt offerings and sin offerings you have taken no pleasure. 7 Then I said, **'Behold, I have come to do your will, O God**, as it is written of me in the scroll of the book.'"
        i. Psalm 40:6-8 - 6 In sacrifice and offering you have not delighted, **but you have given me an open ear**. Burnt offering and sin offering you have not required. 7 Then I said, "Behold, I have come; in the scroll of the book it is written of me: 8 **I delight to do your will, O my God; your law is within my heart**."

    b. Romans 12:1-2 - 1 I appeal to you therefore, brothers, by the mercies of God, to **present your bodies as a living sacrifice, holy and acceptable to God, which is your spiritual worship**. 2 Do not be conformed to this world, but be transformed by the renewal of your mind, that by testing you may **discern what is the will of God, what is good and acceptable and perfect**.

    c. In the Old Testament, lambs and goats and bulls were offered on the altar of sacrifice unto God. Their blood was poured out and their bodies burned to full consumption.
        i. In the New Testament, we offer OURSELVES as the sacrifice, not to literal death but to living in obedience as-if-we-were-dead. Our self will is put to death to do God's will.

2. With our will having been offered on the altar of sacrifice, we are called to slavery to God and to righteousness - what is pleasing to Him.

    a. We have been purchased by God through the blood of Jesus to be set free from sin and death in order to present ourselves to Him as His servants.
        i. 1 Corinthians 7:22-23 - 22 For he who was called in the Lord as a bondservant is a freedman of the Lord. Likewise **he who was free when called is a bondservant of Christ. 23 You were bought with a price**; do not become bondservants of men.
        ii. Romans 6:16-22 - 16 Do you not know that **if you present yourselves to anyone as obedient slaves, you are slaves of the one whom you obey, either of sin, which leads to death, or of obedience, which leads to righteousness?** 17 But thanks be to God, that you who were once slaves of sin have become obedient from the heart to the standard of teaching to which you were committed, 18 and, having been set free from sin, have **become slaves of righteousness**. 19 I am speaking in human terms, because of your natural limitations. For just as you once presented your members as slaves to impurity and to lawlessness leading to more lawlessness, so **now present your members as slaves to righteousness leading to sanctification**. 20 For when you were slaves of sin, you were free in regard to righteousness. 21 But what fruit were you getting at that time from the things of which you are now ashamed? For the end of those things is death. 22 But now that you have been set free from sin and **have become slaves of God**, the fruit you get leads to sanctification and its end, eternal life.

iii. Romans 13:14 - 14 But put on the Lord Jesus Christ, and **make no provision for the flesh, to gratify its desires**.
iv. 2 Corinthians 5:15 - 15 and he died for all, **that those who live might no longer live for themselves but for him** who for their sake died and was raised.

> Slave/Servant: Greek-G1401: *doulos*: 1. A slave, bondman, person of servile condition. 2. A servant or attendant. 3. A slave, literal or figurative, voluntary or involuntary. 4. **One who gives himself up to another's will. Devoted to another to the disregard of one's own interests.**

b. Jesus was a servant of God – even though He was a Son.
   i. Philippians 2:7 - 7 but emptied himself, by **taking the form of a servant**, being born in the likeness of men.
   ii. John 5:19 - 19 So Jesus said to them, "Truly, truly, I say to you, **the Son can do nothing of his own accord**, but only what he sees the Father doing. For whatever the Father does, that the Son does likewise.
   iii. John 5:30 - 30 "**I can do nothing on my own.** As I hear, I judge, and my judgment is just, because **I seek not my own will but the will of him who sent me**.
   iv. John 6:38 - 38 For I have come down from heaven, **not to do my own will but the will of him who sent me**.
   v. John 8:28 - 28 So Jesus said to them, "When you have lifted up the Son of Man, **then you will know that I am he, and that I do nothing on my own authority**, but speak just as the Father taught me.
   vi. John 12:49-50 - 49 For I have not spoken on my own authority, but **the Father who sent me has himself given me a commandment--what to say and what to speak.** 50 And I know that his commandment is eternal life. **What I say, therefore, I say as the Father has told me.**"
   vii. Luke 22:42 - 42 saying, "Father, if you are willing, remove this cup from me. **Nevertheless, not my will, but yours, be done.**"

c. The apostles considered themselves slaves/bondservants of Christ.
   i. Romans 1:1 - 1 **Paul, a servant of Christ Jesus**, called to be an apostle, set apart for the gospel of God,
   ii. 1 Corinthians 4:1 - 1 **This is how one should regard us, as servants of Christ** and stewards of the mysteries of God.
   iii. 1 Corinthians 3:5 - 5 What then is Apollos? What is Paul? **Servants through whom you believed**, as the Lord assigned to each.
   iv. Philippians 1:1 - 1 **Paul and Timothy, servants of Christ Jesus**, To all the saints in Christ Jesus who are at Philippi, with the overseers and deacons:
   v. Titus 1:1 - 1 **Paul, a servant of God** and an apostle of Jesus Christ, for the sake of the faith of God's elect and their knowledge of the truth, which accords with godliness,
   vi. James 1:1 - 1 **James, a servant of God and of the Lord Jesus Christ**, To the twelve tribes in the Dispersion: Greetings.
   vii. 2 Peter 1:1 - 1 **Simeon Peter, a servant** and apostle of Jesus Christ, To those who have obtained a faith of equal standing with ours by the righteousness of our God and Savior Jesus Christ:
   viii. Jude 1:1 - 1 **Jude, a servant of Jesus Christ** and brother of James, To those who are called, beloved in God the Father and kept for Jesus Christ:

3. We are called to be faithful even unto literal death. All are called to death to self. All are called to total obedience to God at the expense of themselves. Some are called to martyrdom.

a. Revelation 2:10 - 10 Do not fear what you are about to suffer. Behold, the devil is about to throw some of you into prison, that you may be tested, and for ten days you will have tribulation. **Be faithful unto death**, and I will give you the crown of life.

b. Revelation 12:11 - 11 And they have conquered him by the blood of the Lamb and by the word of their testimony, **for they loved not their lives even unto death**.

E. The Nature of Love: Laying Down Life for Others in Selfless Mercy

1. Example: Moses reflected the merciful nature of God through his intercession on behalf of Israel. When they failed in the golden calf incident, Moses implored God based on His own mercy, the perspective of their enemies and the nations, and His promises to the patriarchs. God was ready to destroy Israel and start over with Moses but Moses, rather than thinking this was a good thing, interceded for God's people and offered himself in their place.

   a. Exodus 32:9-14 - 9 And the LORD said to Moses, "I have seen this people, and behold, it is a stiff-necked people. 10 Now therefore **let me alone, that my wrath may burn hot against them and I may consume them, in order that I may make a great nation of you.**" 11 **But Moses implored the LORD his God and said, "O LORD, why does your wrath burn hot against your people, whom you have brought out of the land of Egypt with great power and with a mighty hand?** 12 Why should the Egyptians say, 'With evil intent did he bring them out, to kill them in the mountains and to consume them from the face of the earth'? **Turn from your burning anger and relent from this disaster against your people. 13 Remember Abraham, Isaac, and Israel, your servants, to whom you swore by your own self, and said to them, 'I will multiply your offspring as the stars of heaven, and all this land that I have promised I will give to your offspring, and they shall inherit it forever.'"** 14 And the LORD relented from the disaster that he had spoken of bringing on his people.
      i. Then Moses went down to witness the people worshipping the Golden Calf.

   b. Exodus 32:30-32 - 30 The next day Moses said to the people, "You have sinned a great sin. And now I will go up to the LORD; perhaps I can make atonement for your sin." 31 So Moses returned to the LORD and said, "Alas, this people has sinned a great sin. They have made for themselves gods of gold. 32 **But now, if you will forgive their sin--but if not, please blot me out of your book that you have written.**"

2. Example: David erred in taking a census of the people and therefore, God sent a plague of destruction. David asked for the punishment to be on himself and his house rather than on the people who had done no wrong. Historically speaking, the way of pagan kings would be to permit punishment on the people for the preservation of the king. David did the opposite. This is also why David refused to receive as a free gift the place God had commanded for sacrifice to be offered for averting the plague. David was willing to pay any price to petition God for mercy and save God's people. God must be just but He delights to show mercy.

   a. 1 Chronicles 21:16-27 - 16 And David lifted his eyes and saw the angel of the LORD standing between earth and heaven, and in his hand a drawn sword stretched out over Jerusalem. Then David and the elders, clothed in sackcloth, fell upon their faces. 17 And David said to God, "Was it not I who gave command to number the people? It is I who have sinned and done great evil. **But these sheep, what have they done? Please let your hand, O LORD my God, be against me and against my father's house. But do not let the plague be on your**

people." 18 Now the angel of the LORD had commanded Gad to say to David that David should go up and raise an altar to the LORD on the threshing floor of Ornan the Jebusite. 19 So David went up at Gad's word, which he had spoken in the name of the LORD. 20 Now Ornan was threshing wheat. He turned and saw the angel, and his four sons who were with him hid themselves. 21 As David came to Ornan, Ornan looked and saw David and went out from the threshing floor and paid homage to David with his face to the ground. 22 And David said to Ornan, "**Give me the site of the threshing floor that I may build on it an altar to the LORD--give it to me at its full price--that the plague may be averted from the people.**" 23 Then Ornan said to David, "Take it, and let my lord the king do what seems good to him. See, I give the oxen for burnt offerings and the threshing sledges for the wood and the wheat for a grain offering; I give it all." 24 But King David said to Ornan, "No, but I will buy them for the full price. **I will not take for the LORD what is yours, nor offer burnt offerings that cost me nothing.**" 25 So David paid Ornan 600 shekels of gold by weight for the site. 26 And David built there an altar to the LORD and presented burnt offerings and peace offerings and called on the LORD, and the LORD answered him with fire from heaven upon the altar of burnt offering. 27 **Then the LORD commanded the angel, and he put his sword back into its sheath**.

   b. Noteworthy: When Saul was still king, David considered Saul's life to be precious, in spite of the fact that Saul had been terrible and cruel to him.
      i. 1 Samuel 26:21-24 - 21 Then Saul said, "I have sinned. Return, my son David, for I will no more do you harm, **because my life was precious in your eyes this day**. Behold, I have acted foolishly, and have made a great mistake." 22 And David answered and said, "Here is the spear, O king! Let one of the young men come over and take it. 23 The LORD rewards every man for his righteousness and his faithfulness, for the LORD gave you into my hand today, and I would not put out my hand against the LORD's anointed. 24 Behold, **as your life was precious this day in my sight, so may my life be precious in the sight of the LORD**, and may he deliver me out of all tribulation."

   c. Noteworthy: When Absalom opposed David, and conspired against him to take over the kingdom, David wanted his life spared. When Absalom was killed, David wept with his heart broken. So much so that his faithful servants were offended almost to the point of rebellion.
      i. 2 Samuel 18:31-33 - 31 And behold, the Cushite came, and the Cushite said, "**Good news for my lord the king!** For the LORD has delivered you this day from the hand of all who rose up against you." 32 The king said to the Cushite, "Is it well with the young man Absalom?" And the Cushite answered, "May the enemies of my lord the king and all who rise up against you for evil be like that young man." 33 And the king was deeply moved and went up to the chamber over the gate and wept. And as he went, he said, "**O my son Absalom, my son, my son Absalom! Would I had died instead of you, O Absalom, my son, my son!**"
      ii. 2 Samuel 19:5-8 - 5 Then Joab came into the house to the king and said, "You have today covered with shame the faces of all your servants, who have this day saved your life and the lives of your sons and your daughters and the lives of your wives and your concubines, 6 **because you love those who hate you and hate those who love you**. For you have made it clear today that commanders and servants are nothing to you, for today I know that if Absalom were alive and all of us were dead today, then you would be pleased.

3. Example: Jesus knew that all of mankind deserved the wrath of God and eternal torment of hell. But He offered Himself, the righteous for the unrighteous, so that we may receive mercy from God, right standing with Him as a free gift, and peace with Him forevermore. Jesus said, "take me instead of them." He loved us and showed mercy to us, even when we were His enemies.

a. Romans 5:6-10 - 6 For while we were still weak, at the right time **Christ died for the ungodly**. 7 For one will scarcely die for a righteous person--though perhaps for a good person one would dare even to die-- 8 but God shows his love for us in that **while we were still sinners, Christ died for us**. 9 Since, therefore, we have now been justified by his blood, much more shall we be saved by him from the wrath of God. 10 For **if while we were enemies we were reconciled to God by the death of his Son**, much more, now that we are reconciled, shall we be saved by his life.

b. Colossians 1:21-22 NIV - 21 Once you were **alienated from God and were enemies in your minds because of your evil behavior**. 22 But now he has reconciled you by Christ's physical body through death to present you holy in his sight, without blemish and free from accusation

c. 1 John 4:9-10 - 9 In this the love of God was made manifest among us, that **God sent his only Son into the world, so that we might live through him**. 10 In this is love, not that we have loved God but that he loved us and **sent his Son to be the propitiation for our sins**.

d. John 15:13 - 13 Greater love has no one than this, **that someone lay down his life for his friends**.

4. Example: Paul was willing to give his life and salvation in the Lord for the sake of the people of Israel. Paul's burning desire and intercession was for God to take him in their place.

   a. Romans 9:1-5 - 1 I am speaking the truth in Christ--I am not lying; my conscience bears me witness in the Holy Spirit-- 2 that **I have great sorrow and unceasing anguish in my heart**. 3 **For I could wish that I myself were accursed and cut off from Christ for the sake of my brothers, my kinsmen according to the flesh**. 4 They are Israelites, and to them belong the adoption, the glory, the covenants, the giving of the law, the worship, and the promises. 5 To them belong the patriarchs, and from their race, according to the flesh, is the Christ, who is God over all, blessed forever. Amen.

5. Example: Us – true Christian believers and followers of Jesus. God is after a heart of love like His. We are called to lay down our lives through love by dying to ourselves daily for the benefit of others so that they may know and experience the love of Christ through our lives.

   a. 1 John 3:16 - 16 By this we know love, that he laid down his life for us, and **we ought to lay down our lives for the brothers**.

   b. 1 Corinthians 13:4-8a - 4 Love is patient and kind; love does not envy or boast; it is not arrogant 5 or rude. It does not insist on its own way; it is not irritable or resentful; 6 it does not rejoice at wrongdoing, but rejoices with the truth. 7 Love bears all things, believes all things, hopes all things, endures all things. 8 Love never ends.

   c. Matthew 5:43-48 - 43 "You have heard that it was said, 'You shall love your neighbor and hate your enemy.' 44 But I say to you, **Love your enemies and pray for those who persecute you,** 45 **so that you may be sons of your Father who is in heaven.** For he makes his sun rise on the evil and on the good, and sends rain on the just and on the unjust. 46 For if you love those who love you, what reward do you have? Do not even the tax collectors do the same? 47 And if you greet only your brothers, what more are you doing than others? Do not even the Gentiles do the same? 48 **You therefore must be perfect [mature], as your heavenly Father is perfect [mature]**.

d. Luke 6:27-36 - 27 "But I say to you who hear, **Love your enemies, do good to those who hate you**, 28 **bless those who curse you, pray for those who abuse you**. 29 To one who strikes you on the cheek, offer the other also, and from one who takes away your cloak do not withhold your tunic either. 30 Give to everyone who begs from you, and from one who takes away your goods do not demand them back. 31 **And as you wish that others would do to you, do so to them**. 32 "If you love those who love you, what benefit is that to you? For even sinners love those who love them. 33 And if you do good to those who do good to you, what benefit is that to you? For even sinners do the same. 34 And if you lend to those from whom you expect to receive, what credit is that to you? Even sinners lend to sinners, to get back the same amount. 35 **But love your enemies, and do good, and lend, expecting nothing in return, and your reward will be great, and you will be sons of the Most High**, for he is kind to the ungrateful and the evil. 36 **Be merciful, even as your Father is merciful**.

www.manifestinternational.com

Other Courses Available or Coming Soon:
Cornerstone: Foundations of the Faith
Perfection: Towards Spiritual Maturity
Parables of Jesus
God's Economics
Humble Yourself: The Way to Greatness
The Gospel is the Power
Jews, Israel, & Jesus
The Obedience of Faith

More to Follow...

www.ingramcontent.com/pod-product-compliance
Lightning Source LLC
Chambersburg PA
CBHW080445110426
42743CB00016B/3281